Art of Inspiration
Words to Live By

S.J. Bauer

Table of Contents

Introduction
The Art of Inspiration Project

Several years ago, I decided it might be interesting to incorporate a word within my geometric designs in such a way that the word was partially concealed within the overall composition. The intention was that one should be able to look at the painting and be drawn to it without realizing a word was there. The word and/or message that I was trying to convey would therefore be of a somewhat subliminal nature. The words I chose were mostly inspirational or motivational in tone.

As these new paintings began to collect in my studio, I noticed that they seemed to play off one another resulting in a very dramatic and powerful amplification of positive energy. The energy of the whole exceeded that of the individual works of art. Words indeed have power. Collectively, they have more power.

I decided that I should keep these paintings together in a collection that could be shown to the public. That show is now comprised of over 50 paintings. The goal is to provide a beautiful and inspirational show that can uplift the viewer and provoke thoughtful contemplation about what these words and phrases mean and how they relate to an increasingly polarized society. Do these words mean the same thing to people of differing political views, religious views, or social classes? On a more global scale, do these words have the same significance to a person in Pakistan as they do to a person in the United States? In most cases, the answer is yes.

It is very easy to marginalize a political opponent, or a religion, or a race, or gender, or even an entire nation, based on superficial information gleaned from quick news clips on social media and mainstream news outlets. In these times where news is delivered through social media tailored to one's personal profile, we find ourselves in an echo chamber where opposing ideas and views are excluded. In such a world it is easy to imagine that our views are the only "right" views and anything that opposes these views is wrong and potentially evil. Engagement with opposing views or people is seen as betrayal of one's moral character, friends, and core beliefs. However, if one looks a bit deeper and casts aside such superficial views, it is easy to see that these snap characterizations are misleading, and in most cases, completely false.

In my travels of the world, I have found that people everywhere are pretty much the same. They worry about the same basic things we do, such as job security, food, shelter, personal safety, education of children, love, health, and a dignified existence. This exposition challenges viewers to think about what these words mean to them and then visualize how they think people of different ethnicities, different religions, different political beliefs, or living in different places in the world might view these same words. Are the meanings and significance the same? Hopefully, the end result of this thought exercise will be a fresh outlook on the things that connect us as a species rather than those that differentiate us. The things that connect us are more powerful and reflect what makes us human. All the rest is simply window dressing. We need to be mindful that the person we disagree with has ideas born of his or her personal experience. Different does not necessarily mean wrong. Different experience equals different ideas. Right or wrong is simply a matter of perspective. If you cannot convincingly argue the opposing viewpoint, you do not understand the problem.

When I conceived this idea of the Art of Inspiration Project, I wanted to appeal to society on a more spiritual level. At the spiritual level people are connected in a very fundamental way. Whether we realize it or not, the words we use, spoken or not, send energy rippling out into our surroundings, and this energy reflects back to us in kind. Positive energy reflects back in a positive way, and negative energy reflects back in a negative manner. We can all think of examples where we were kind to someone and that kindness was similarly returned. When we smile at someone, that smile will be returned. When we strike out at someone in anger, that anger will be returned.

What we think and say matters. The words we choose form our own actions as well as the actions of those around us. In a world that seems increasingly confrontational, chaotic, and negative, we need to be mindful that we can physically alter ourselves and our surroundings by simply thinking and speaking in a different way. Buddha is quoted as saying "All that we are is a result of what we have thought," meaning that we create our own world, our own destiny, and our own way of life, simply through the power of thought. What we think determines our actions. If we think positive things, our actions will be positive, and this positively affects the thoughts and actions of those around us. We can literally change the world by thought alone. This book, and the live art exhibit it is based on, is intended to provide a fun, beautiful, and intellectually challenging way to project our thoughts in a positive direction. This positive energy is infectious and will directly affect those around us. The benefit to society as a whole is obvious.

In laying out this book, the words are not presented in any particular order of importance. The layout was chosen to mix up the various style differences for the purpose of making the book flow better visually. In each case, the painting is displayed on the right and the title, size, and material composition of the original painting is on the left facing page. I also included quotes about the word that were inspirational to me and provide a hint of what I had in mind in choosing that particular word. The titles of the paintings provide hints about what word is hidden in the painting without actually telling you what it is. I did this to make the viewer have to work a bit to figure out the words. After all, that is half the fun. Once you figure out what the word in the painting is, you will find that the entire character of the painting changes and the word that was difficult to see at first becomes prominent. Once seen, it cannot be unseen. I provided an index of paintings in the back of the book that tells what each of the words are in case you get stumped. Be forewarned, there is one painting in the group that contains a word in Hebrew which only a few people will be able to decipher.

In the live exhibition of this art, there is an interactive feature where viewers are encouraged to write their own thoughts on these words and their applicability to a global society. I wanted to provide a way to transfer this interactivity to the written book. To accomplish this I provided a couple lines at the bottom of each quote page to provide a space for you, the owner of the book, to pen your own quote or thoughts about the word in the adjacent painting. It is my hope that this will make the book a uniquely personal object where you become a part of the narrative. It will make you think about these words more deeply. Having to come up with your own definition or inspirational quote will require you to consider the impact of these words more deeply as they apply to yourself and humanity as a whole. I see this as an almost meditative exercise that will prove highly valuable to those who chose to do it. It will be something you can look back on, like a school yearbook, to see where your head was at in this particular point in time or provide your children or grandchildren with an inside peek into your thought processes and what kind of person you were long after you are gone. These things cannot be readily gleaned from piles of travel pictures and family photos we traditionally leave behind.

The last section of the book describes a charity project I just completed as this book was in its final stages of production. I wanted to do a wall mural for charity incorporating some inspirational word that was appropriate for the selected venue. I chose SafeNest, which is an abused women and children's shelter here in Clark County, Nevada. SafeNest provides a variety of services including secure shelters for victims of domestic violence and their children as well as court assistance, counseling, and community outreach activities. I chose the word "Hope" as I felt this was the one thing that everyone who entered their shelter had in common. This mural project was an amazing experience for me in having the opportunity to meet some of these women and get to know a little about them and their stories. Please read about this exciting project, the people involved, and the results that were achieved starting on page 107.

I hope you find this book uplifting and personally useful. Feel free to drop me an email through my website (sjbauer.com) telling me what you think, positive or negative, about this book and the concept I created within. I would love to know how this book affected you.

With warmest regards,
Scott J. Bauer
www.sjbauer.com

About The Artist

I never thought of myself as an artist. I was not one who was prone to doodling or sketching. The last time I picked up a paintbrush was in grade school watercolor class. So it seems strange to me that at this point in my life I find myself making a living producing art.

Throughout my life I was driven by one insatiable need, to acquire new knowledge and new skills. I wanted to know what made things tick. Everything from protons and neutrons to mechanical devices, to the rise and fall of civilizations. Even as a child I had an annoying habit of disassembling my new toys within a day or two of receiving them, much to my parents dismay.

Along the way I have been a builder, a mechanic, a teacher, a gardener, a pilot, a restauranteur, a scientist, an engineer, an inventor, an entrepreneur, a writer, a philosopher, a historian, a traveler, a student of the human condition, and now, an artist. I have become the quintessential Renaissance man in every definition of the word.

Looking back, I realize that there was always an element of art in everything I did. I just did not understand it as such. My art reflects many aspects of the things done in my life. I see things in terms of straight lines, perfectly round circles, solid colors, and hard edges. When ideas come to me, they come in the form of two dimensional images, perfectly drawn. I live in a world consisting of circles, squares, triangles, lines, and arcs. There seems to be an almost spiritual purity in the things I create.

Pythogoras, the father of geometry started a religion based on geometry and the perfection of mathematics as the language of the universe. In like manner, I see perfection in these basic forms and create works of art based on combinations of primitive shapes and colors to produce compositions that stimulate both the analytical and emotional sides of the brain.

No two people see exactly the same thing in my art. Like looking at clouds, what you see depends entirely on your own visual perception. I am not above leading the viewer a bit though. I cannot resist the temptation to throw in numbers, symbols, mathematical relationships, and other hidden tidbits drawn from the many things I have done in my life. Why I did what I did and what it all means depends on your particular point of view. There are no wrong answers. I leave it to the critics and art scholars to label it and figure it all out. In the mean time, I will go happily on my way exploring the myriad ways I might titillate the senses with simple shapes, vivid colors, and interesting compositions. The possibilities are endless.

Can't We All Just Get Along?

"We will only begin to forgive when we can look upon the wrongdoers as ourselves, neither better nor worse. We need to remember that we coexist as mortals in the world, together, the wronged and the wrongdoer, and that, in our common humanity, the situation could readily be reversed."
Leo Buscaglia

"In these times, in this harsh, rude, warring world that we live in, where most of the bloodshed is 'My god is greater than your god,' and we're fighting in the name of our god, we have to find a way to peaceably coexist, spiritually."
Vera Farmiga

"The only alternative to coexistence is codestruction."
Jawaharlal Nehru

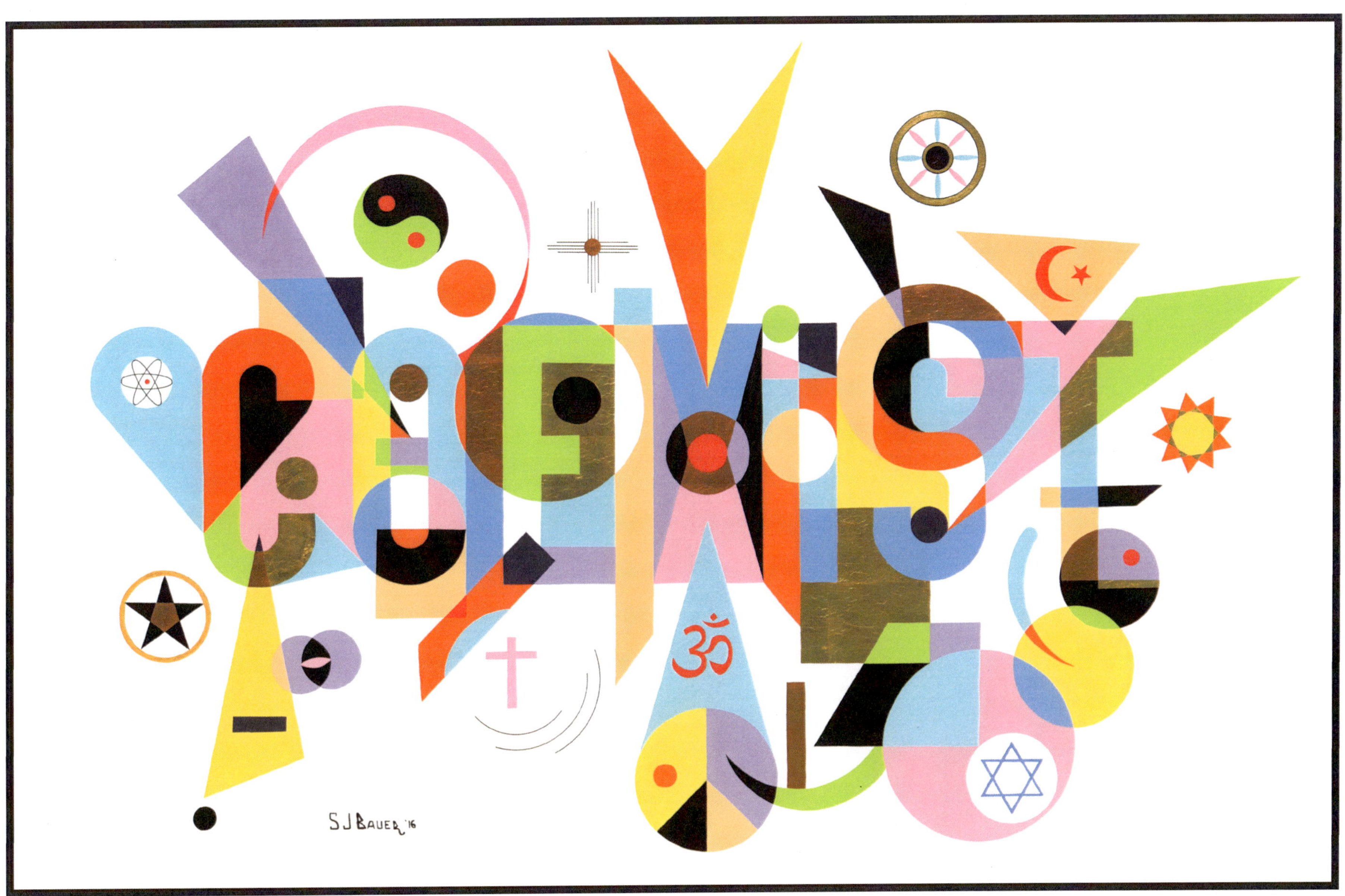

COEXIST
SJBAUER '16

Living Life in Peace

24" x 30" Mixed media on canvas

"Imagine all the people living life in peace. You, you may say I'm a dreamer, but I'm not the only one. I hope some day you'll join us and the world will be as one."
John Lennon

"If you can imagine it, you can achieve it. If you can dream it, you can become it."
William Arthur Ward

"Whatever you vividly imagine, ardently desire, sincerely believe, and enthusiastically act upon ... must inevitably come to pass."
Paul Meyer

"Imagine, and it shall be. There are no limits."
Evelyn Skye

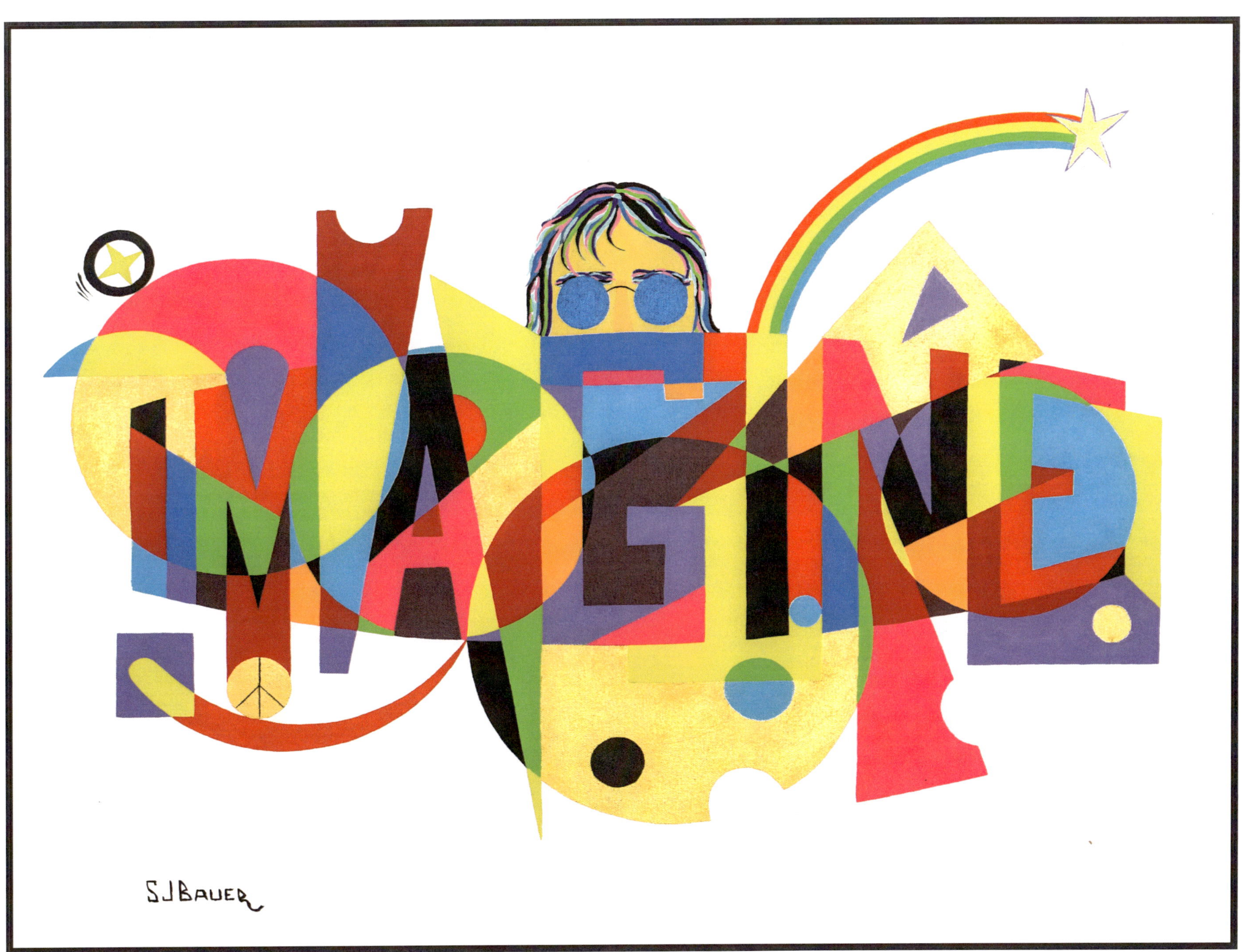

IMAGINE
SJBAUER

Reason to Carry On

36" x 36" Acrylic on canvas

"Hope is being able to see that there is light despite all of the darkness."
Desmond Tutu

"No matter what sort of adversity or challenge you might face, you can always believe that, with hope, it can be conquered and, in the end, you will be stronger for it."
Brooke Ellison

"If you lose hope, somehow you lose the vitality that keeps moving, you lose that courage to be, that quality that helps you go on in spite of it all. And so today I still have a dream."
Martin Luther King Jr.

"Hope is the power of being cheerful in circumstances that we know to be desperate."
G.K. Chesterton

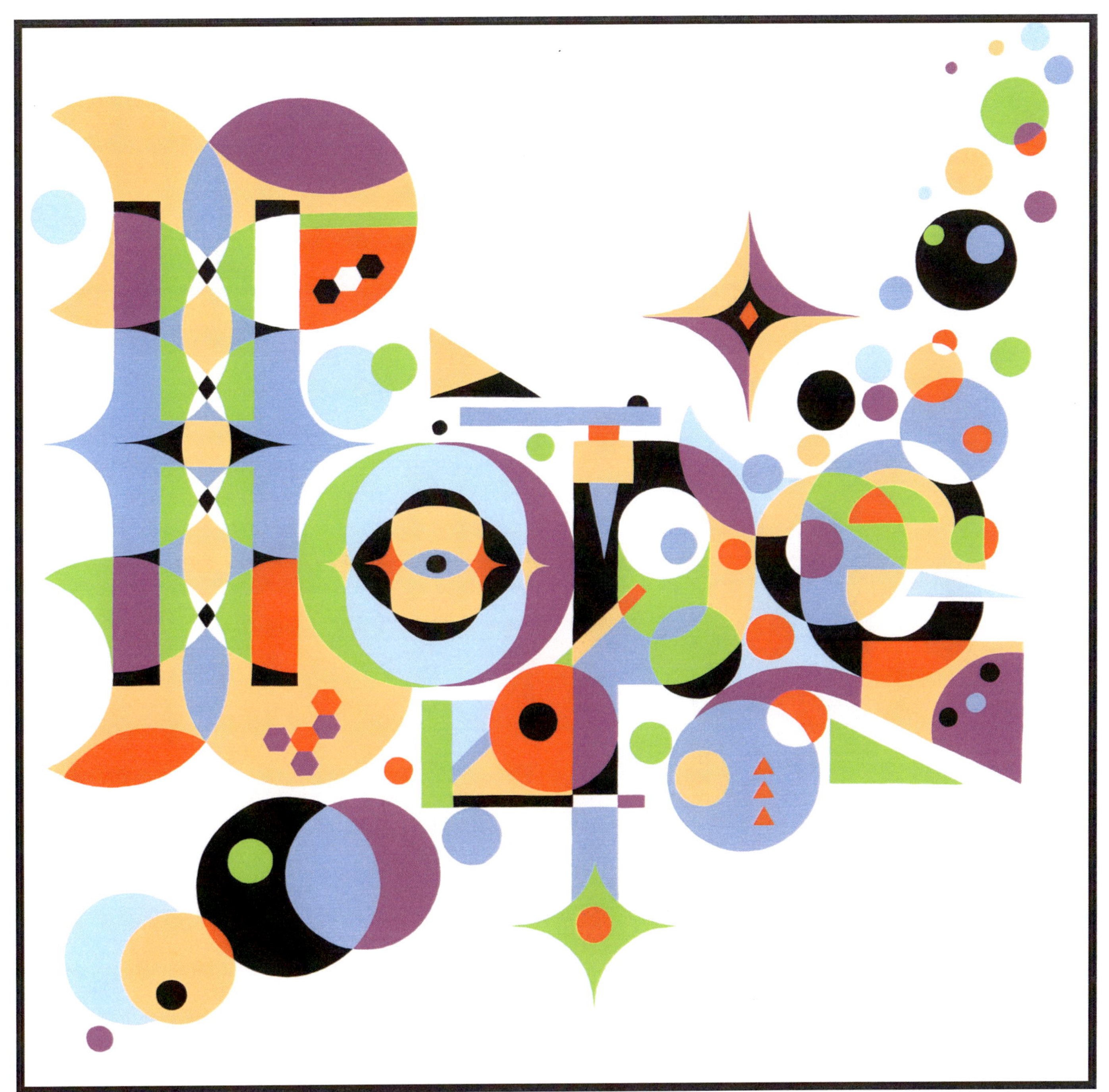
Hope

Let it Grow

36" x 36" Acrylic on canvas

"One day you will ask me which is more important? My life or yours? I will say mine and you will walk away not knowing that you are my life."
Khalil Gibran

"Immature love says: 'I love you because I need you.' Mature love says 'I need you because I love you.'"
Erich Fromm

"Being deeply loved by someone gives you strength while loving someone deeply gives you courage."
Lao Tzu

"We always believe our first love is our last, and our last love our first."
George W. Melville

"You come to love not by finding the perfect person, but by seeing an imperfect person perfectly."
Sam Keen

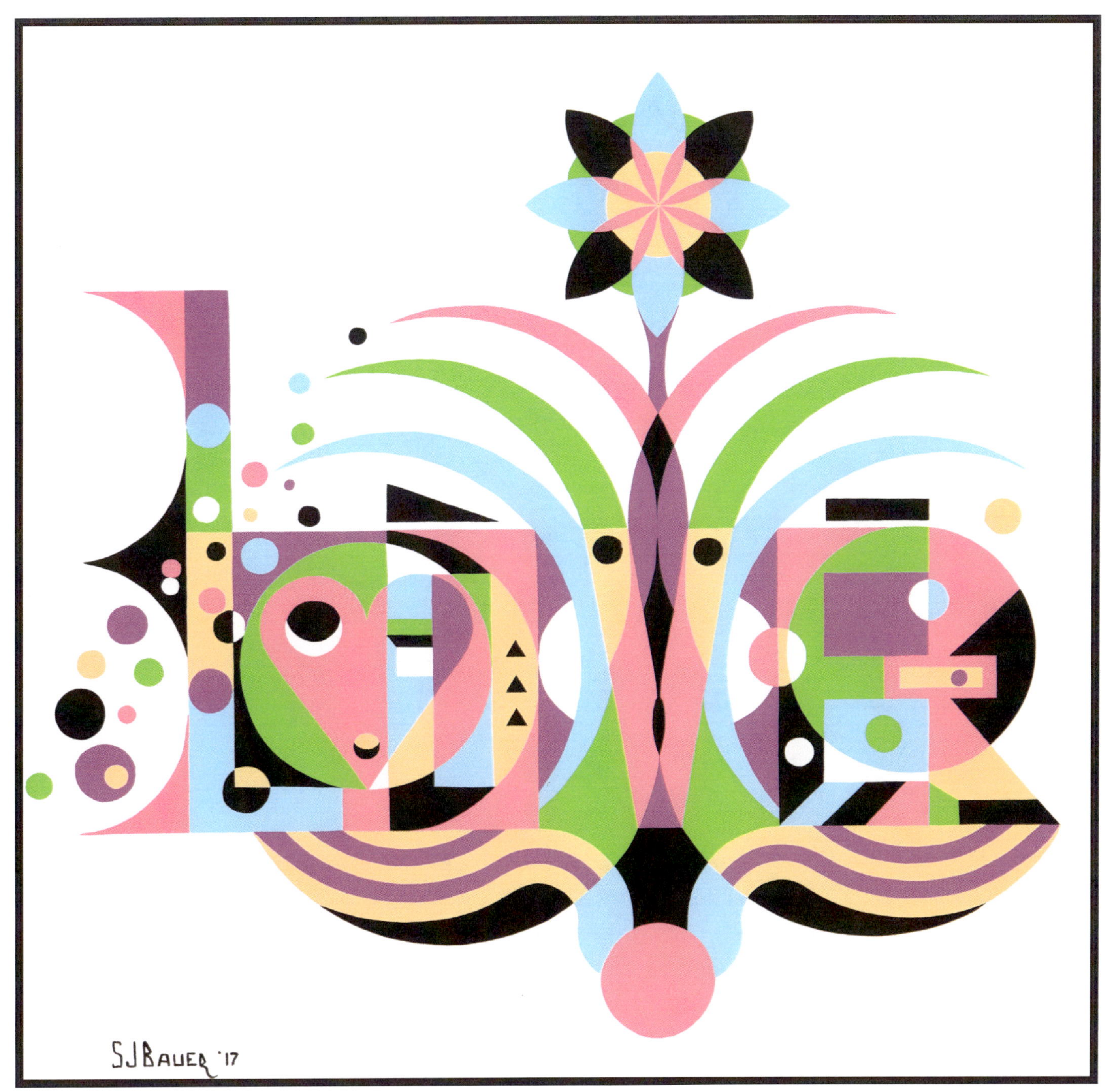

SJBauer '17

Comes From Within

24" x 36" Mixed media on canvas

"When I was 5 years old, my mother always told me that happiness was the key to life. When I went to school, they asked me what I wanted to be when I grew up. I wrote down 'happy'. They told me I didn't understand the assignment. I told them they didn't understand life."
John Lennon

"Happiness doesn't depend on what we have, but it does depend on how we feel toward what we have. We can be happy with little and miserable with much."
William D. Hoard

"When one door of happiness closes, another opens, but often we look so long at the closed door that we do not see the one that has been opened for us."
Helen Keller

"Happiness is when what you think, what you say, and what you do are in harmony."
Mahatma Gandhi

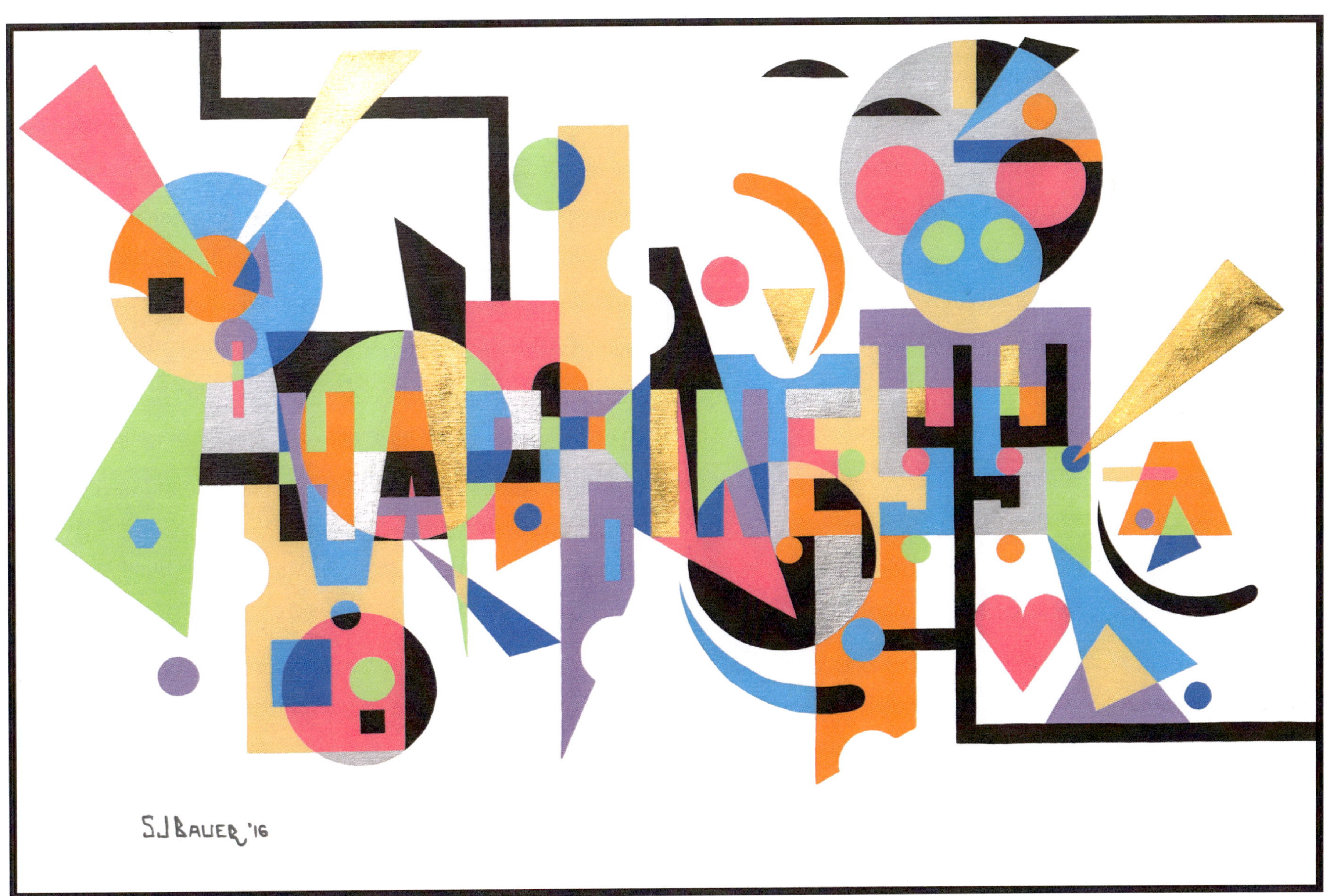

SJ BAUER '16

What Would Jesus Do?

24" x 36" Mixed media on canvas

"Forgiveness is the fragrance that the violet sheds on the heel that has crushed it."
Mark Twain

"Because I make mistakes, I know others do too. I've found when I give forgiveness, it's me - not the other person - who benefits."
Ellen Miller

"Forgiveness is a powerful thing. It doesn't change what has happened; it changes what is to come."
Janeen Latini

"Unforgiveness is like having weeds in the garden of our soul. Weeds grow and reproduce until an entire garden is destroyed. If you want a garden of love, joy, and peace in your heart, you must get rid of all the weeds."
Patricia Partney Dascher

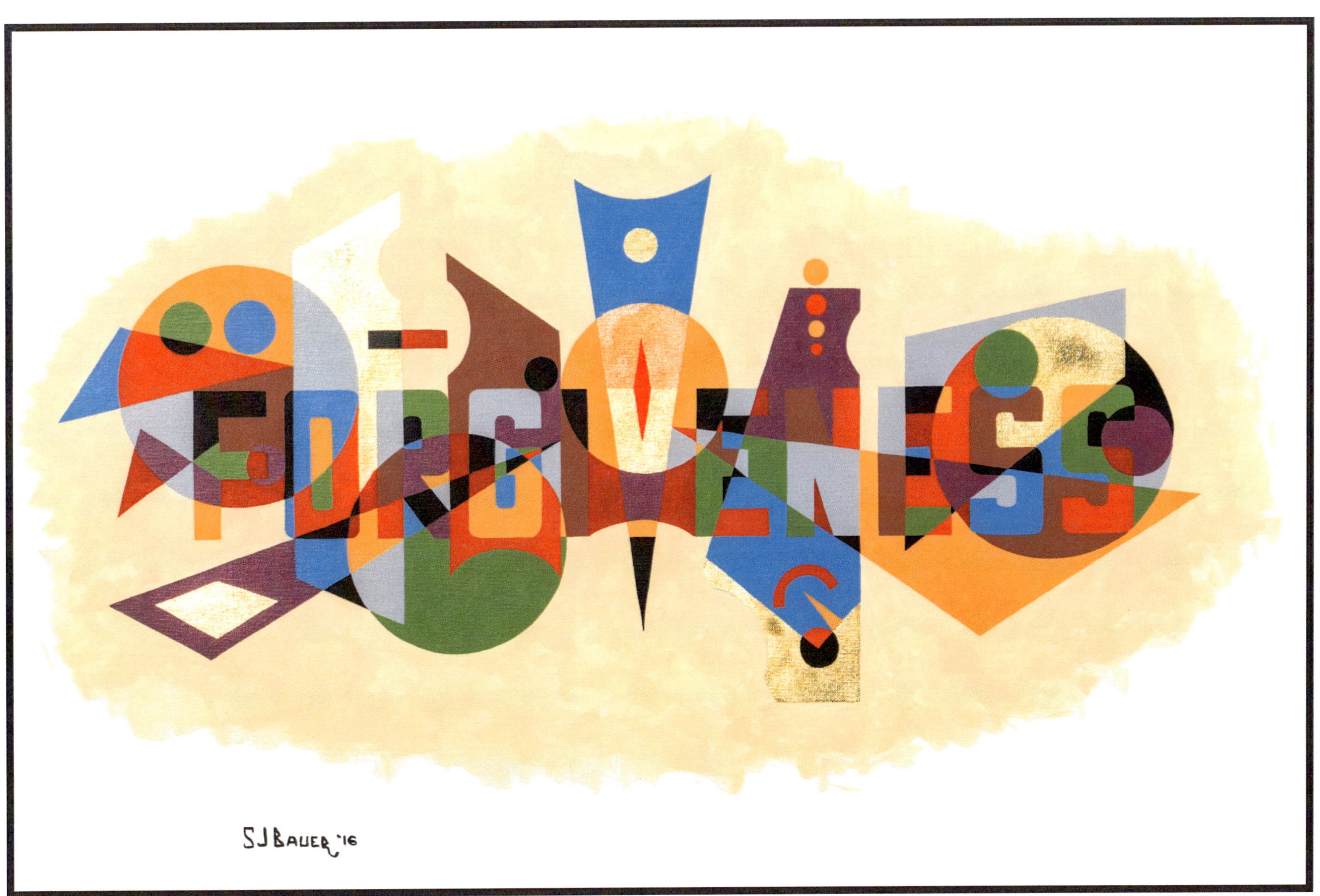

FORGIVENESS
SJ BAUER '16

It's a Thorny Subject

24" x 30" Mixed media on canvas

"If you want peace, you don't talk to your friends. You talk to your enemies."
Desmond Tutu

"We do not inherit the earth from our ancestors; we borrow it from our children"
Chief Seattle

"Peace cannot be achieved through violence; it can only be attained through understanding."
Ralph Waldo Emerson

"Peace is not simply the absence of violence; it is the cultivation of understanding, insight, and compassion, combined with action."
Thich Nhat Hanh

"I believe that as soon as people want peace in the world they can have it. The trouble is they are not aware they can get it. "
John Lennon

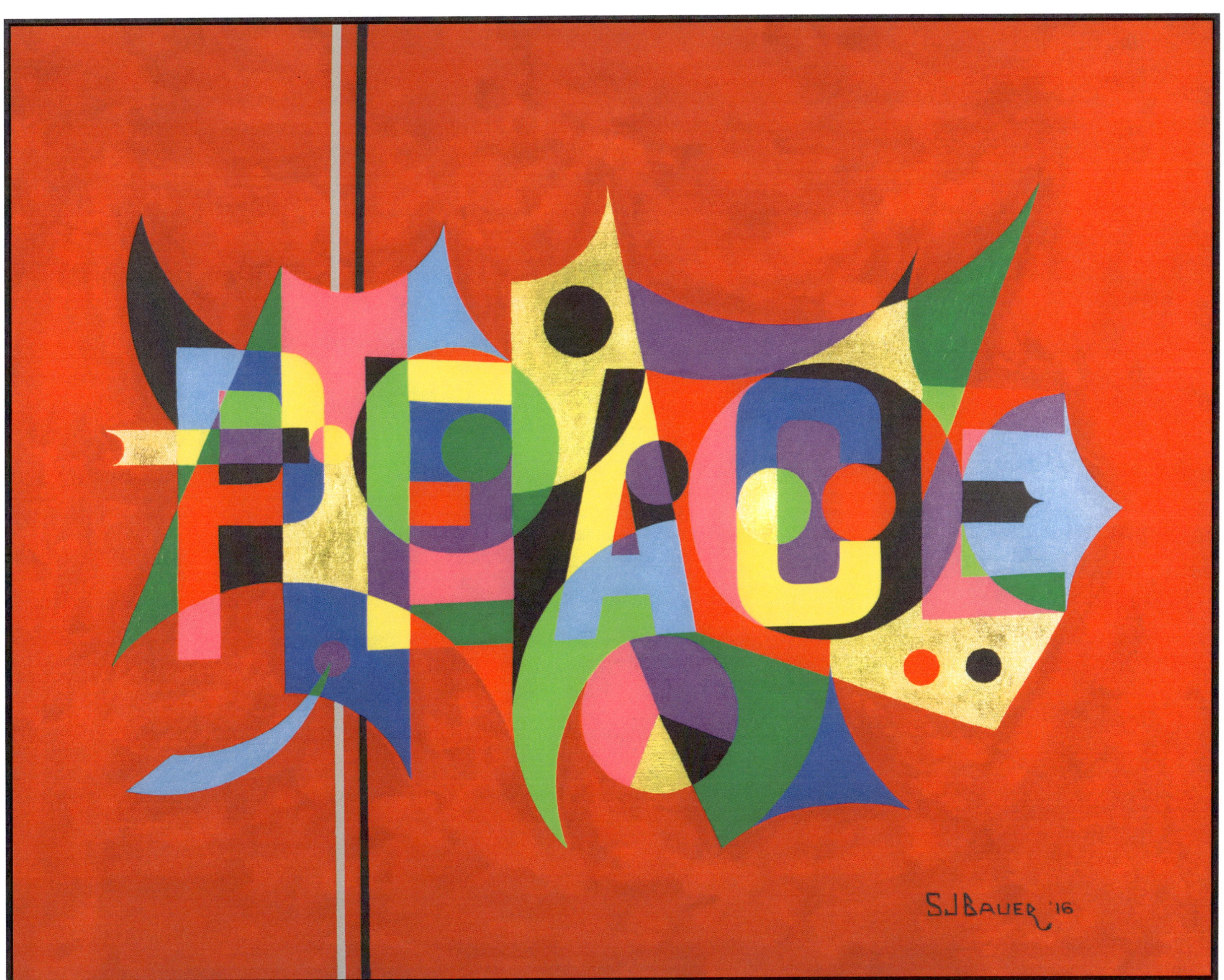

PEACE
SJ BAUER '16

No Kidding

24" x 24" Mixed media on canvas

"All truth passes through three stages. First, it is ridiculed. Second, it is violently opposed. Third, it is accepted as being self-evident."
Arthur Schopenhauer

"Anyone who doesn't take truth seriously in small matters cannot be trusted in large ones either."
Albert Einstein

"Stop hanging out with people that tell you what you want to hear. Hang out with people who tell you the truth."
Eric Thomas

"In a time of deceit telling the truth is a revolutionary act."
George Orwell

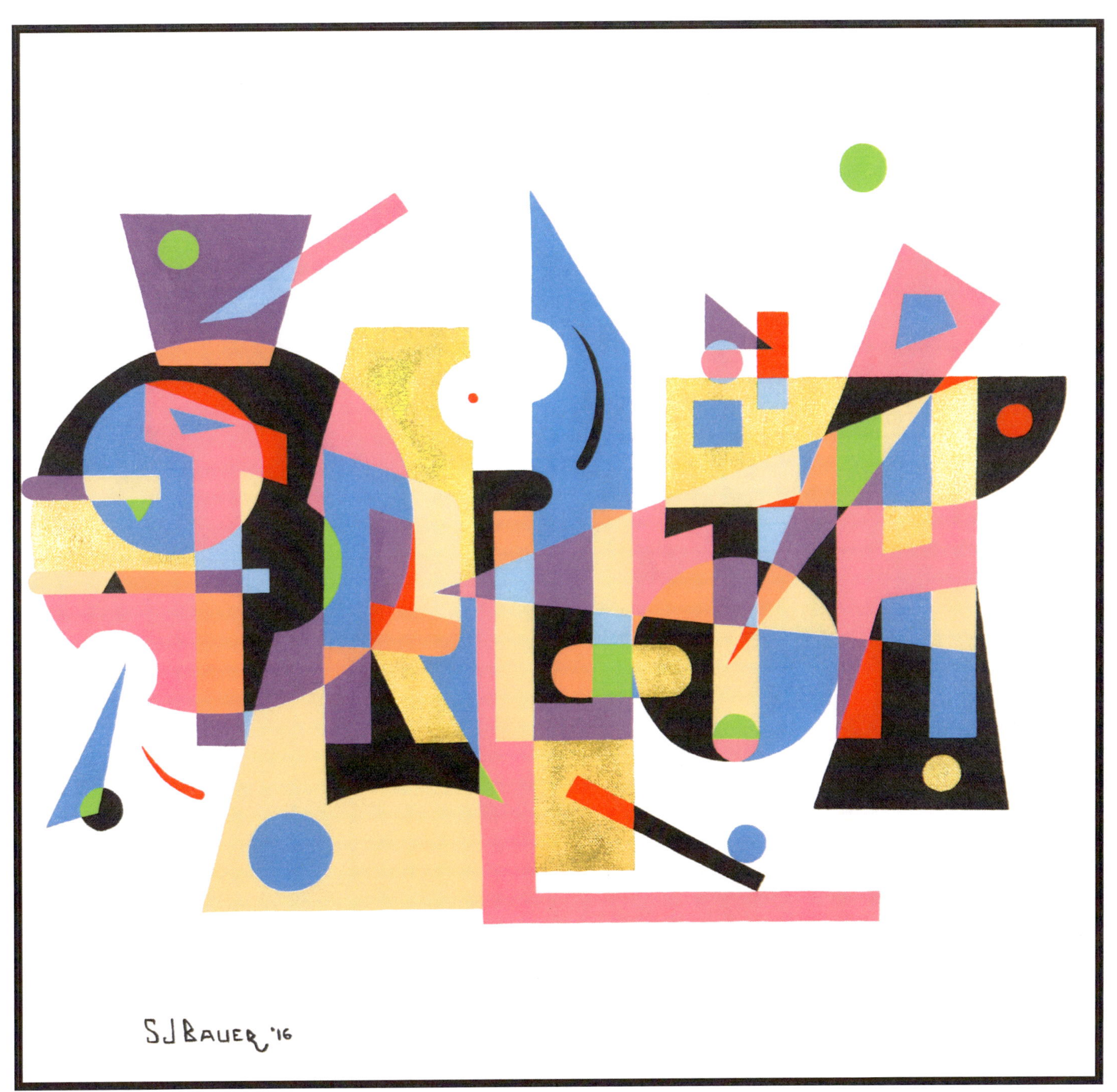
SJ BAUER '16

Give it Up

24" x 30" Mixed media on canvas

"We make a living by what we get, but we make a life by what we give."
Winston Churchill

"Charity isn't about pity, it is about love."
Mother Teresa

"The difference between a helping hand and an outstretched palm is a twist of the wrist."
Laurence Leamer

"Charity is injurious unless it helps the recipient to become independent of it."
John D. Rockefeller

"A bone to the dog is not charity. Charity is the bone shared with the dog, when you are just as hungry as the dog."
Jack London

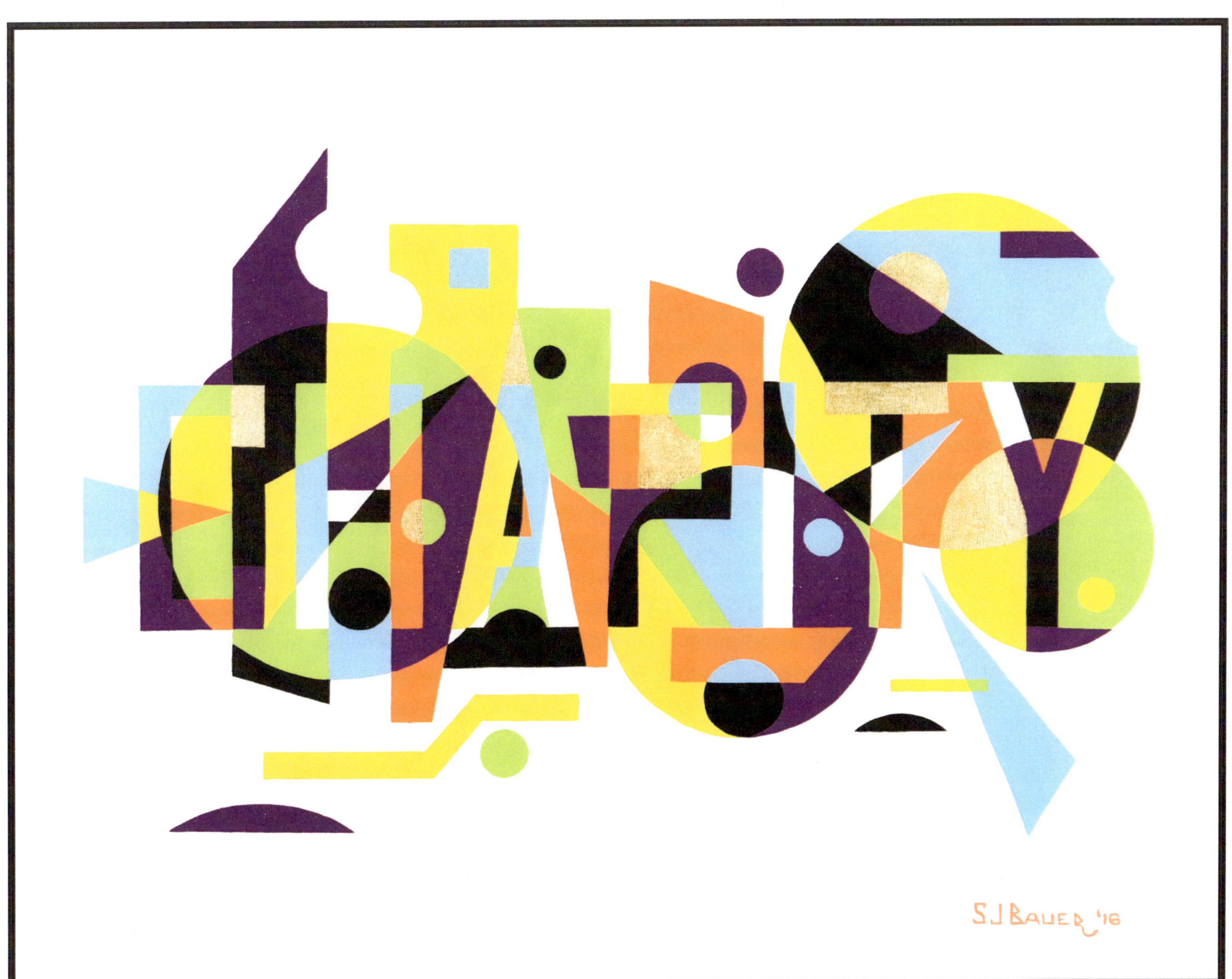

HAPPY
SJ BAUER '16

I Believe

30" x 30" Mixed media on canvas

"To one who has faith, no explanation is necessary. To one without faith, no explanation is possible."
Thomas Aquinas

"Faith is taking the first step even when you don't see the whole staircase."
Martin Luther King, Jr.

"In the affairs of this world, men are saved not by faith, but by the want of it."
Benjamin Franklin

"Every tomorrow has two handles. We can take hold of it with the handle of anxiety or the handle of faith".
Henry Ward Beecher

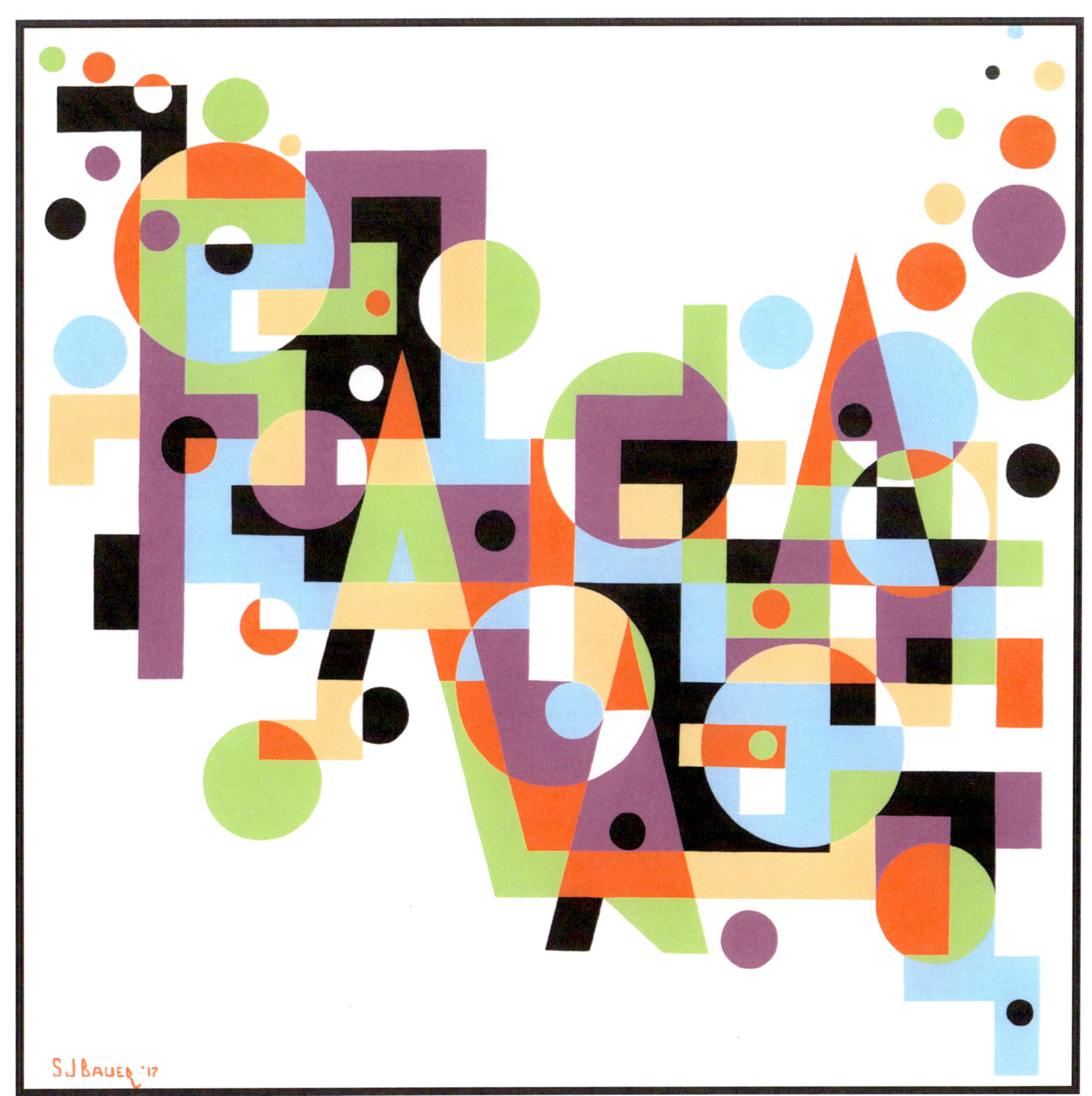

It's Not Free

30" x 40" Acrylic on canvas

"Freedom is never voluntarily given by the oppressor; it must be demanded by the oppressed."
Martin Luther King, Jr.

"Those who profess to favor freedom, and yet depreciate agitation, are men who want crops without plowing up the ground."
Frederick Douglass

"The only real prison is fear, and the only real freedom is freedom from fear."
Aung San Suu Kyi

"For to be free is not merely to cast off one's chains, but to live in a way that respects and enhances the freedom of others."
Nelson Mandela

"In the truest sense, freedom cannot be bestowed; it must be earned."
Franklin D. Roosevelt

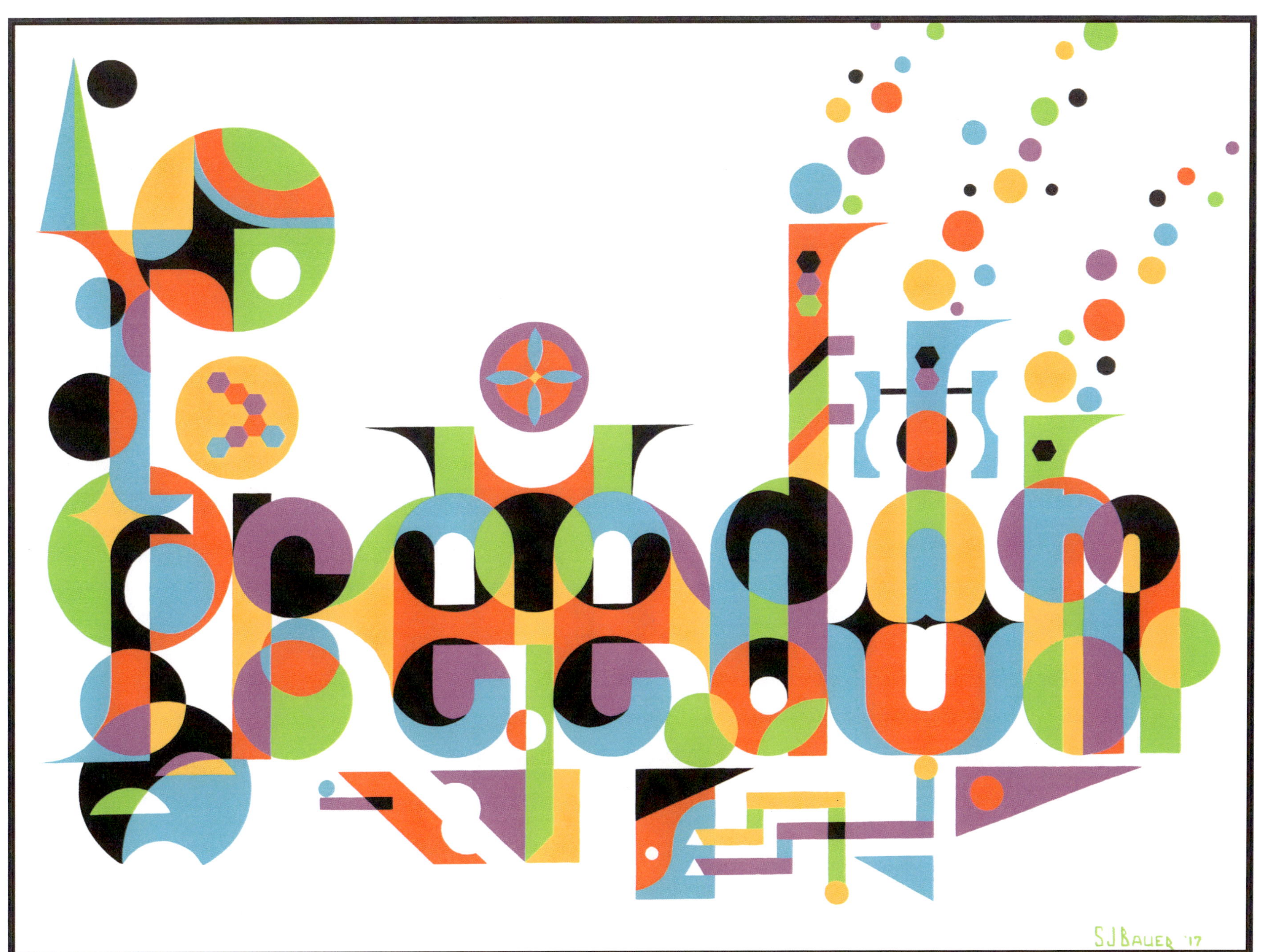
SJ Bauer '17

Depression

24" x 24" Acrylic on canvas

"If you know someone who's depressed, please resolve never to ask them why. Depression isn't a straightforward response to a bad situation; depression just is, like the weather. Try to understand the blackness, lethargy, hopelessness, and loneliness they're going through. Be there for them when they come through the other side. It's hard to be a friend to someone who's depressed, but it is one of the kindest, noblest, and best things you will ever do."
Stephen Fry

"That terrible mood of depression of whether it's any good or not is what is known as The Artist's Reward."
Ernest Hemingway

"It is very hard to explain to people who have never known serious depression or anxiety the sheer continuous intensity of it. There is no off switch."
Matt Haig

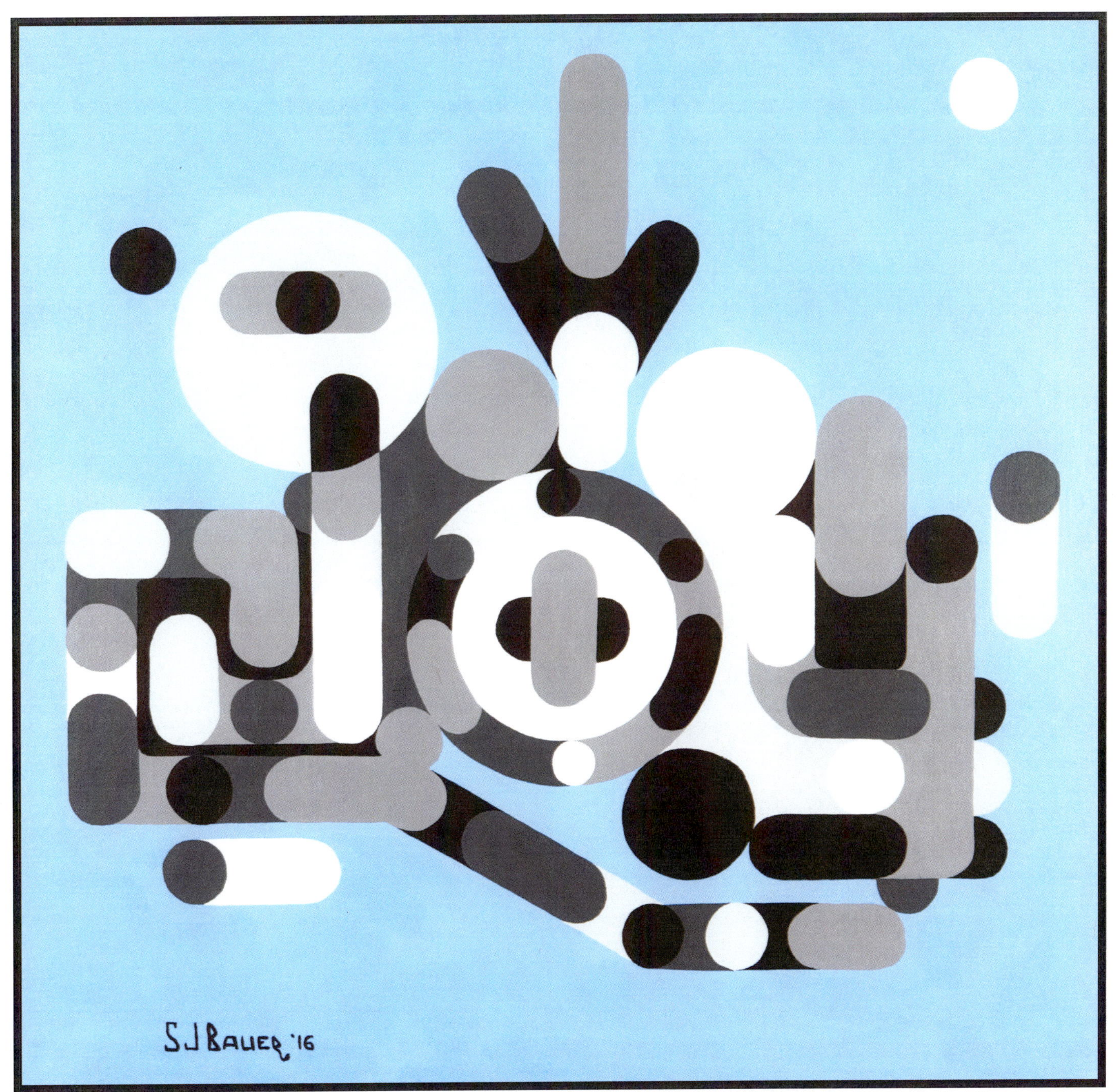

SJ Bauer '16

This is What Will Happen

48" x 60" Acrylic on canvas

"Act as if what you intend to manifest in life is already a reality. Eliminate thoughts of conditions, limitations, or the possibility of it not manifesting. If left undisturbed in your mind and in the mind of intention simultaneously, it will germinate in the physical world."
Wayne Dyer

"Your intentions are your nonphysical causes that set energy into motion. They create a multitude of effects and, therefore, determine the experiences of your life. This is one of the most important things that you can know. It is also something that you can see for yourself is true."
Gary Zukav

"When you left the house today, you had the intention of putting clothes on and you did. You didn't try to put your pants on today. You simply put them on. The same has to hold for all of our intentions. We don't try to be more loving partners. We make the intention, and we act on it."
Patch Adam

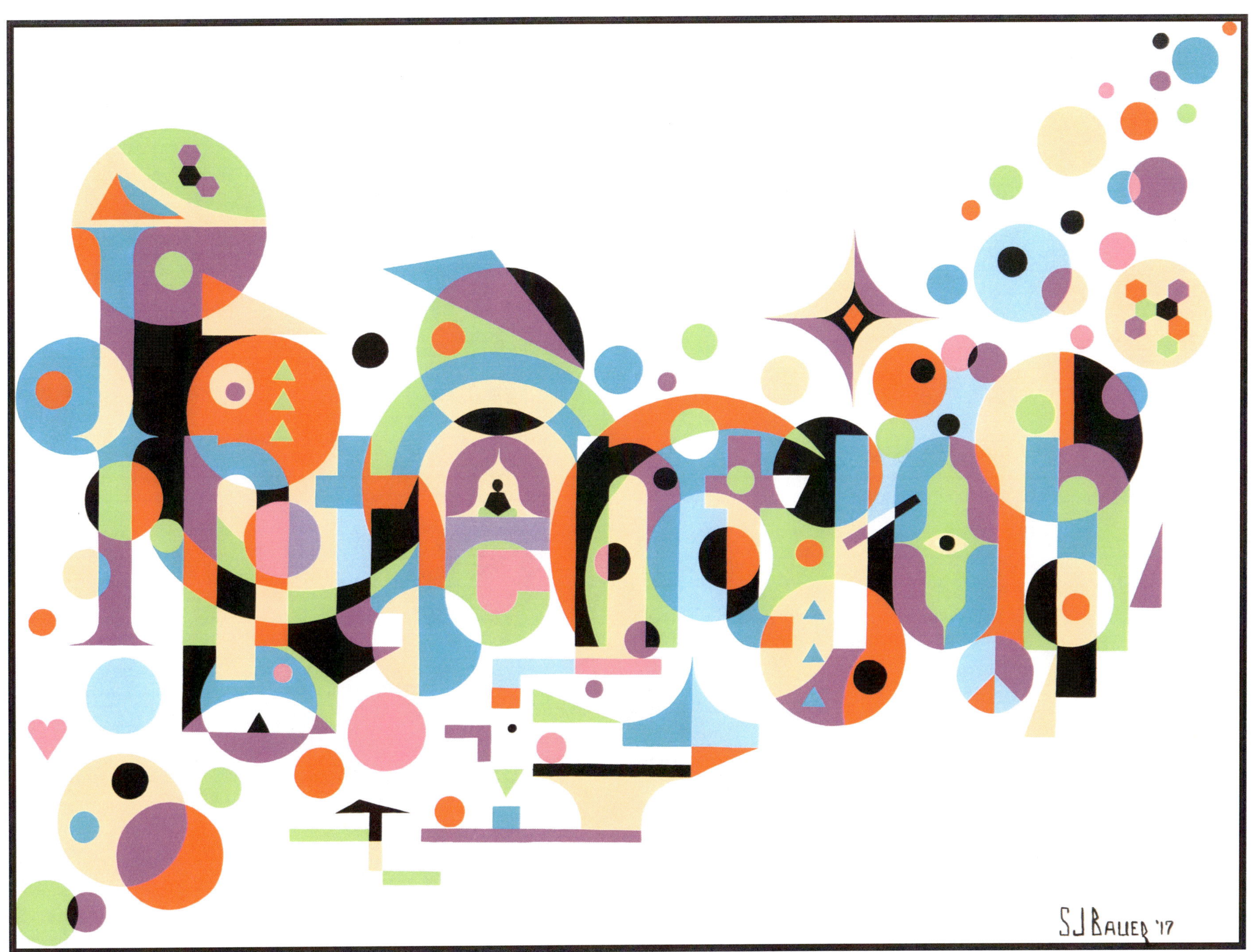

You Have a Brain

30" x 30" Acrylic on canvas

"Be yourself and think for yourself, and while your conclusions may not be infallible they will be nearer right than the inclusions forced upon you by those who have a personal interest in keeping you in ignorance."
Elbert Hubbard

"It is better to keep your mouth closed and let people think you are a fool than to open it and remove all doubt."
Mark Twain

"We are shaped by our thoughts; we become what we think. When the mind is pure, joy follows like a shadow that never leaves."
Buddha

"The function of education is to teach one to think intensively and to think critically. Intelligence plus character - that is the goal of true education."
Martin Luther King, Jr.

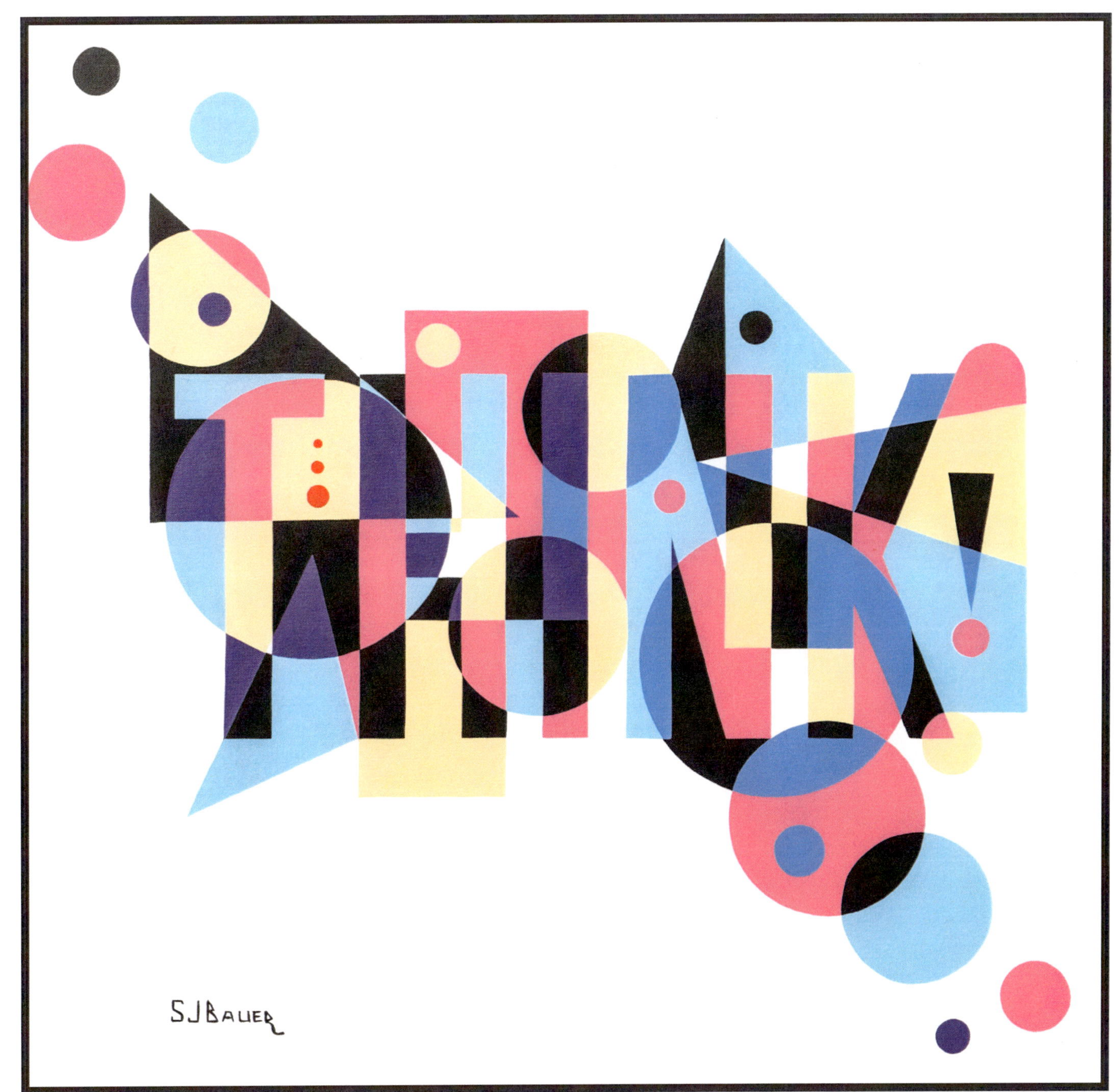

THINK!
THINK!
SJBAUER

Cut it Out Eh?

30" x 40" Mixed media on canvas

*"There's no honorable way to kill, no gentle way to destroy.
There is nothing good in war. Except its ending."*
Abraham Lincoln

"I believe in compulsory cannibalism. If people were forced to eat what they killed, there would be no more wars."
Abbie Hoffman

"Violence and arms can never resolve the problems of men."
Pope John Paul II

"I hate war as only a soldier who has lived it can, only as one who has seen its brutality, its futility, its stupidity."
Dwight D. Eisenhower

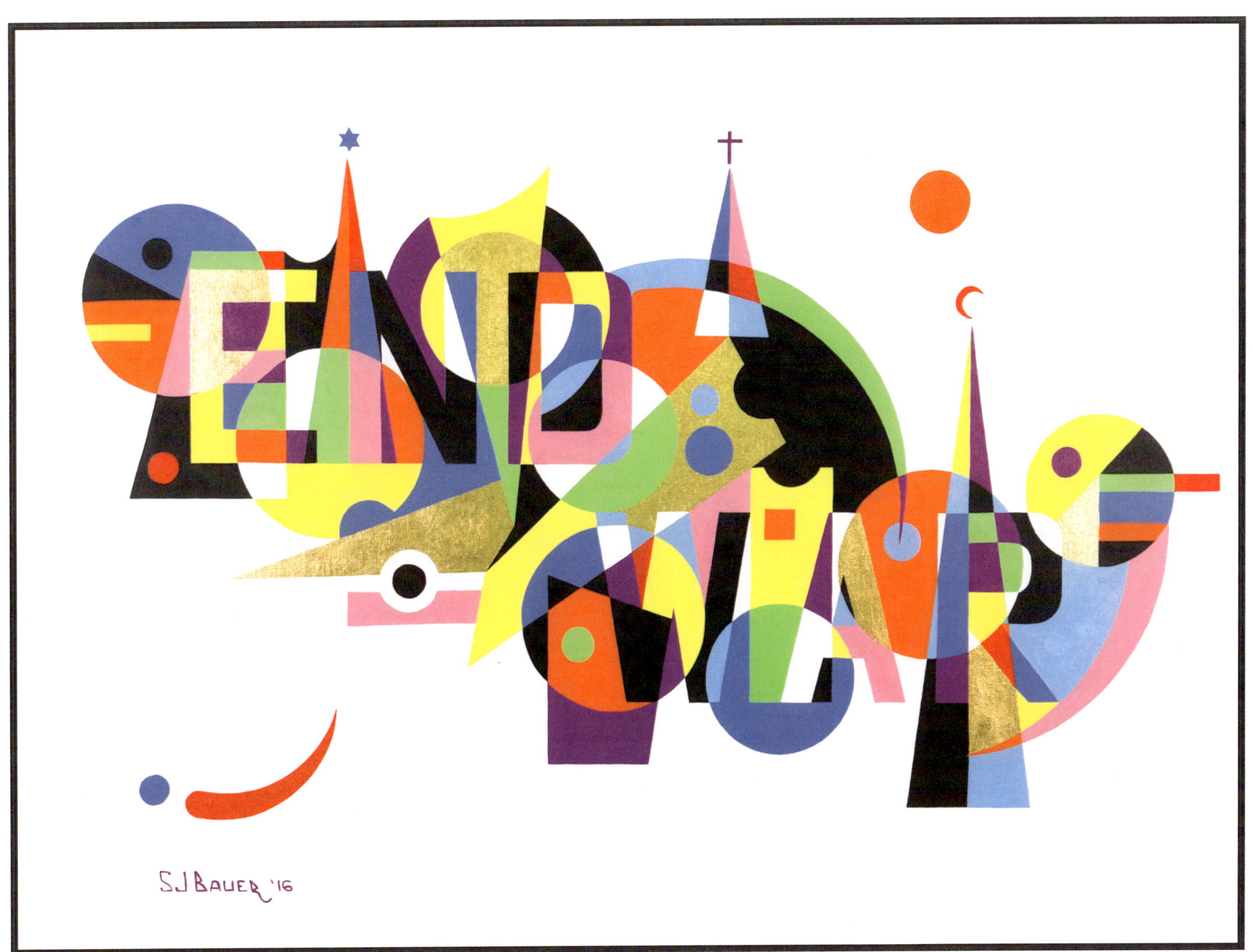

END WARS
SJ BAUER '16

Boldly Go

30" x 40" Mixed media on canvas

"Transcending the world does not mean to withdraw from the world, to no longer take action, or to stop interacting with people. Transcendence of the world is to act and to interact without any self-seeking."
Eckhart Tolle

"Your body is not who you are. The mind and spirit transcend the body."
Christopher Reeve

"Within ourselves, there are voices that provide us with all the answers that we need to heal our deepest wounds, to transcend our limitations, to overcome our obstacles or challenges, and to see where our soul is longing to go."
Debbie Ford

"Only conscious man can mirror the universal: he can consciously become one with the universal and so can consciously transcend the individual."
Piet Mondrian

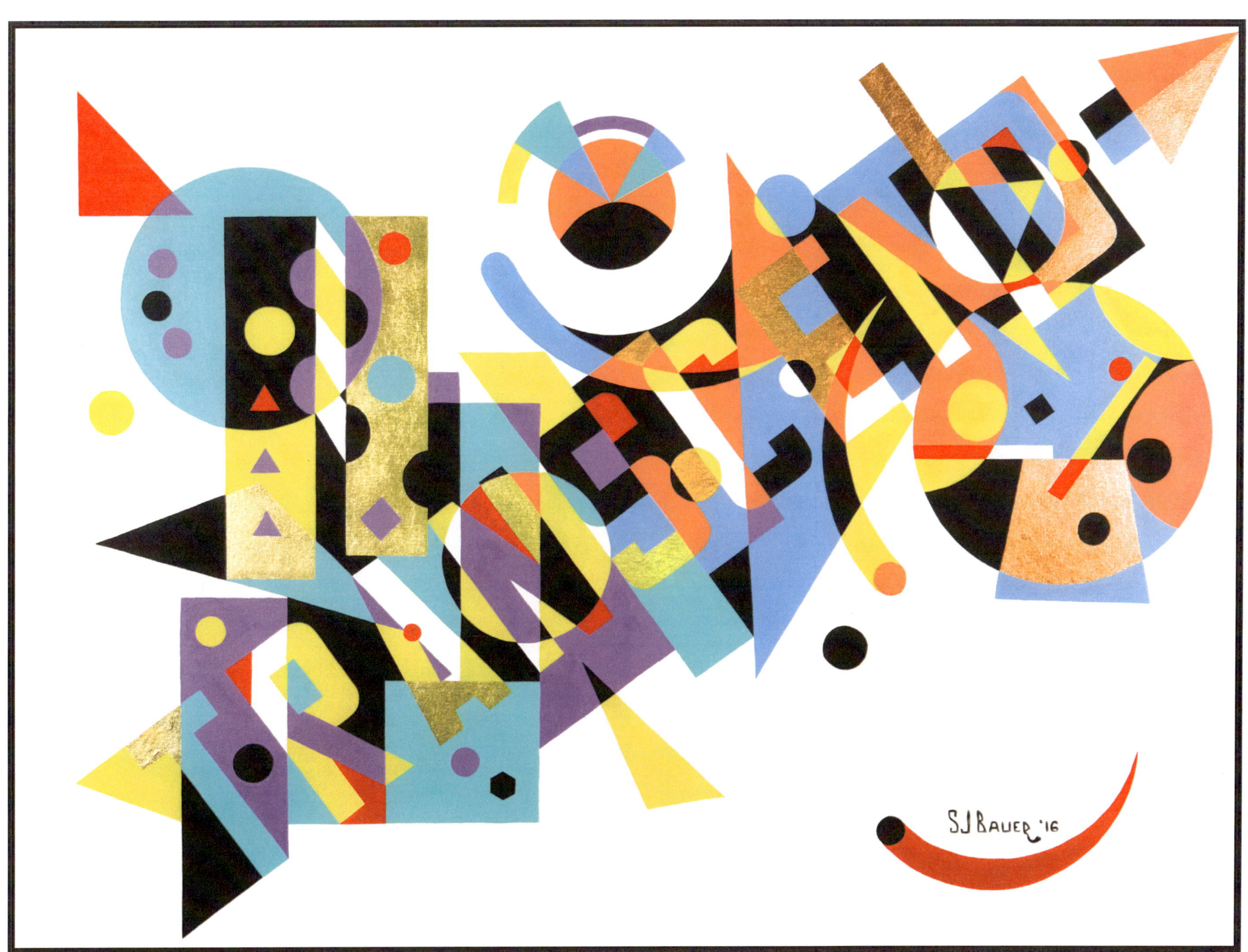

Do the Right Thing

24" x 30" Acrylic on canvas

"He has honor if he holds himself to an ideal of conduct though it is inconvenient, unprofitable, or dangerous to do so."
Walter Lippmann

"It is better to deserve honors and not have them than to have them and not deserve them."
Mark Twain

"Always demanding the best of oneself, living with honor, devoting one's talents and gifts to the benefits of others - these are the measures of success that endure when material things have passed away."
Henry Ford

"Duty, Honor, Country. Those three hallowed words reverently dictate what you ought to be, what you can be, what you will be."
Douglas MacArthur

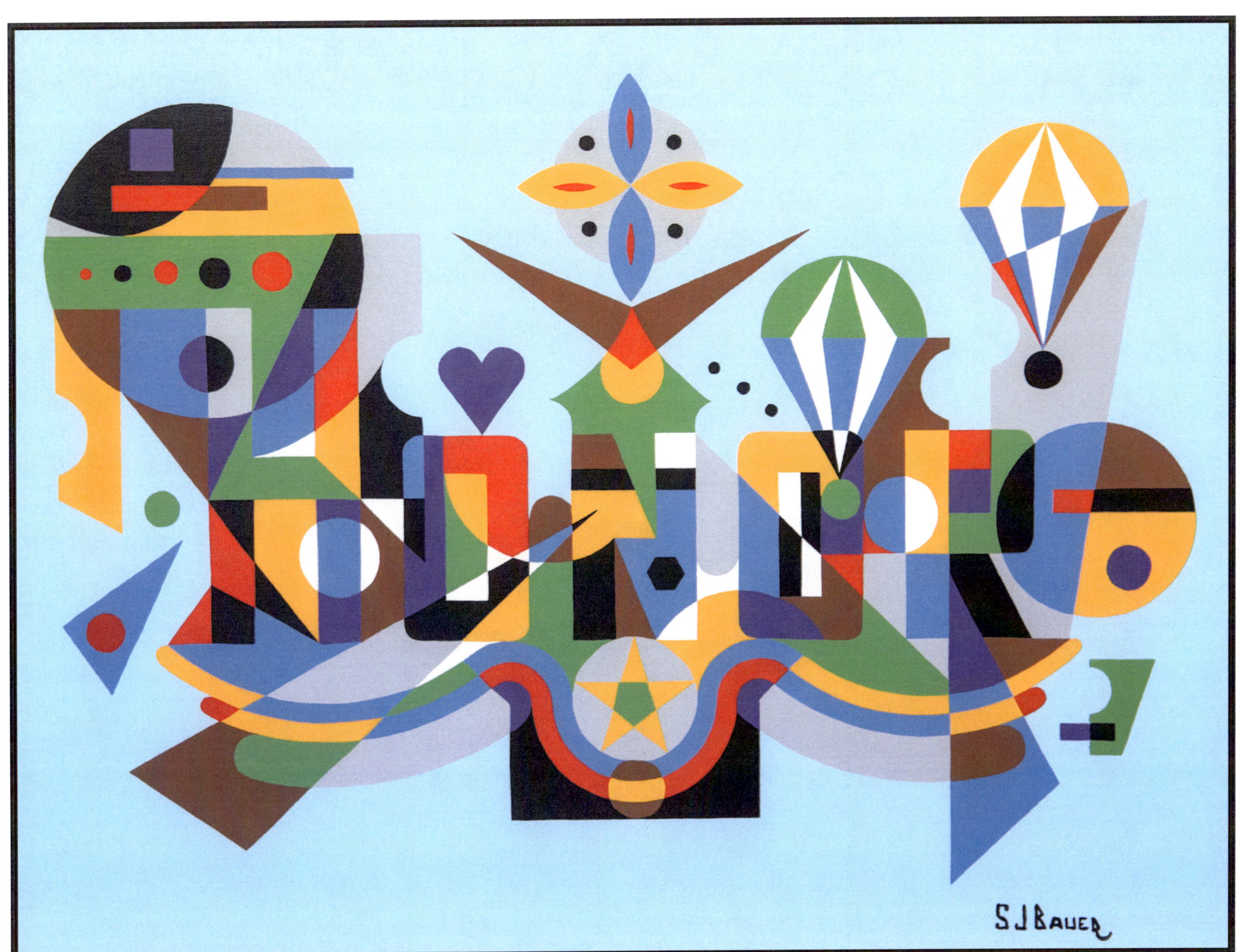

SJ Bauer

Bow to the Spirit Within

30" x 40" Mixed media on canvas

"In India when we meet and part we often say, "Namaste," which means: I honor the place in you where the entire universe resides; I honor the place in you of love, of light, of truth, of peace. I honor the place within you where if you are in that place in you and I am in that place in me, there is only one of us... "Namaste."
Ram Dass

"Namaste is a term that finds its origin in India means the God in me salutes the God in you. This means that every human being has a God in her or him. I wonder where in time we forgot this wisdom and started treating fellow human beings as untouchables and backward classes."
Jeroninio Almeida

There is the house whose people sit in darkness; dust is their food and clay is their meat. They are clothed like birds with wings for covering, they see no light, they sit in darkness. I entered the house of dust and I saw the kings of the earth, their crowns put away for ever."
Anonymous

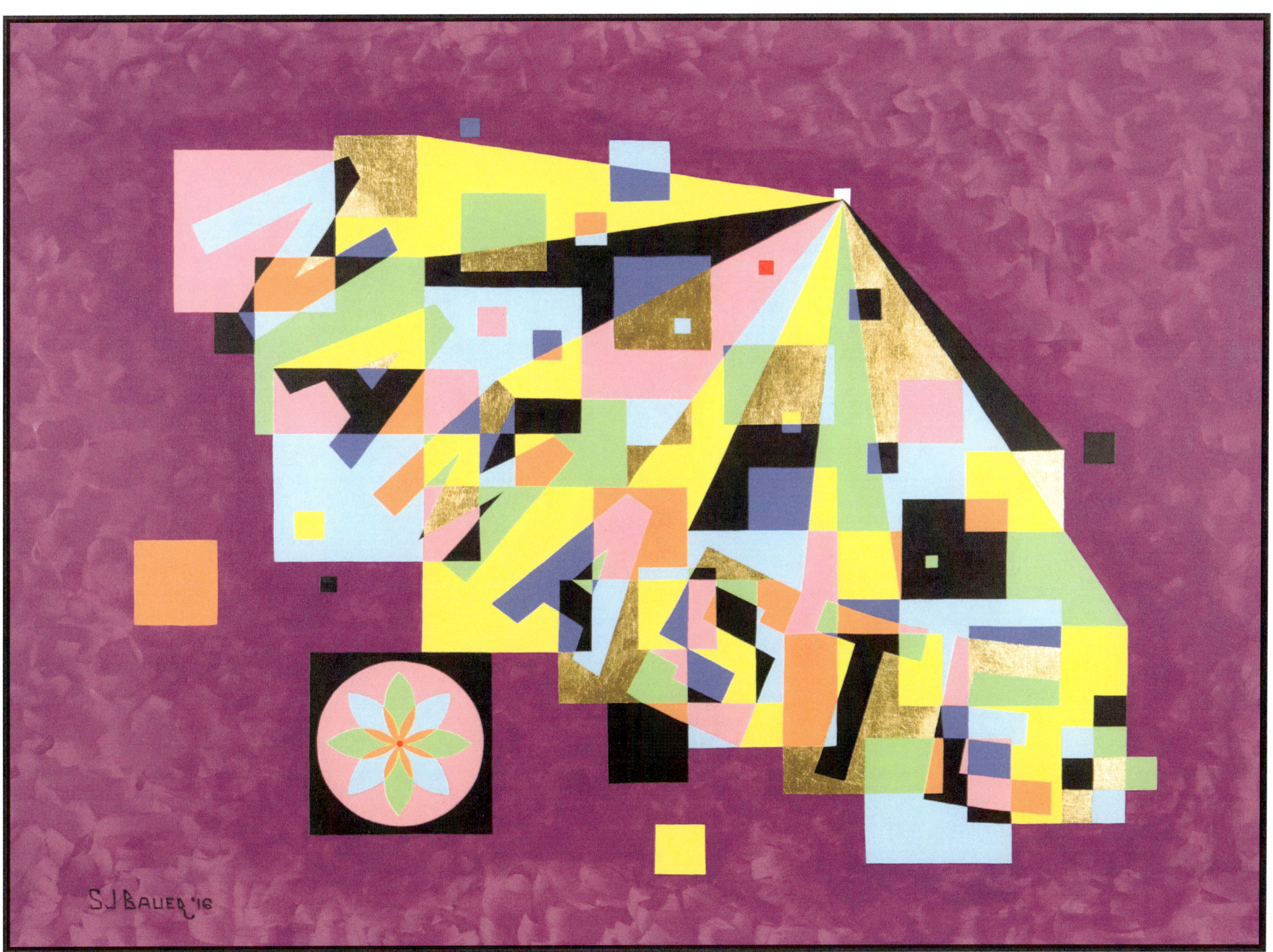

SJ Bauer '16

You Can Do Anything

30" x 40" Acrylic on canvas

"If you believe it will work out , you'll see opportunities. If you believe it won't you will see obstacles."
Wayne Dyer

"Some people say I have attitude - maybe I do... but I think you have to. You have to believe in yourself when no one else does - that makes you a winner right there."
Venus Williams

"Believe in yourself! Have faith in your abilities! Without a humble but reasonable confidence in your own powers you cannot be successful or happy."
Norman Vincent Peale

"Whatever you want in life, other people are going to want it too. Believe in yourself enough to accept the idea that you have an equal right to it."
Diane Sawyer

____

____

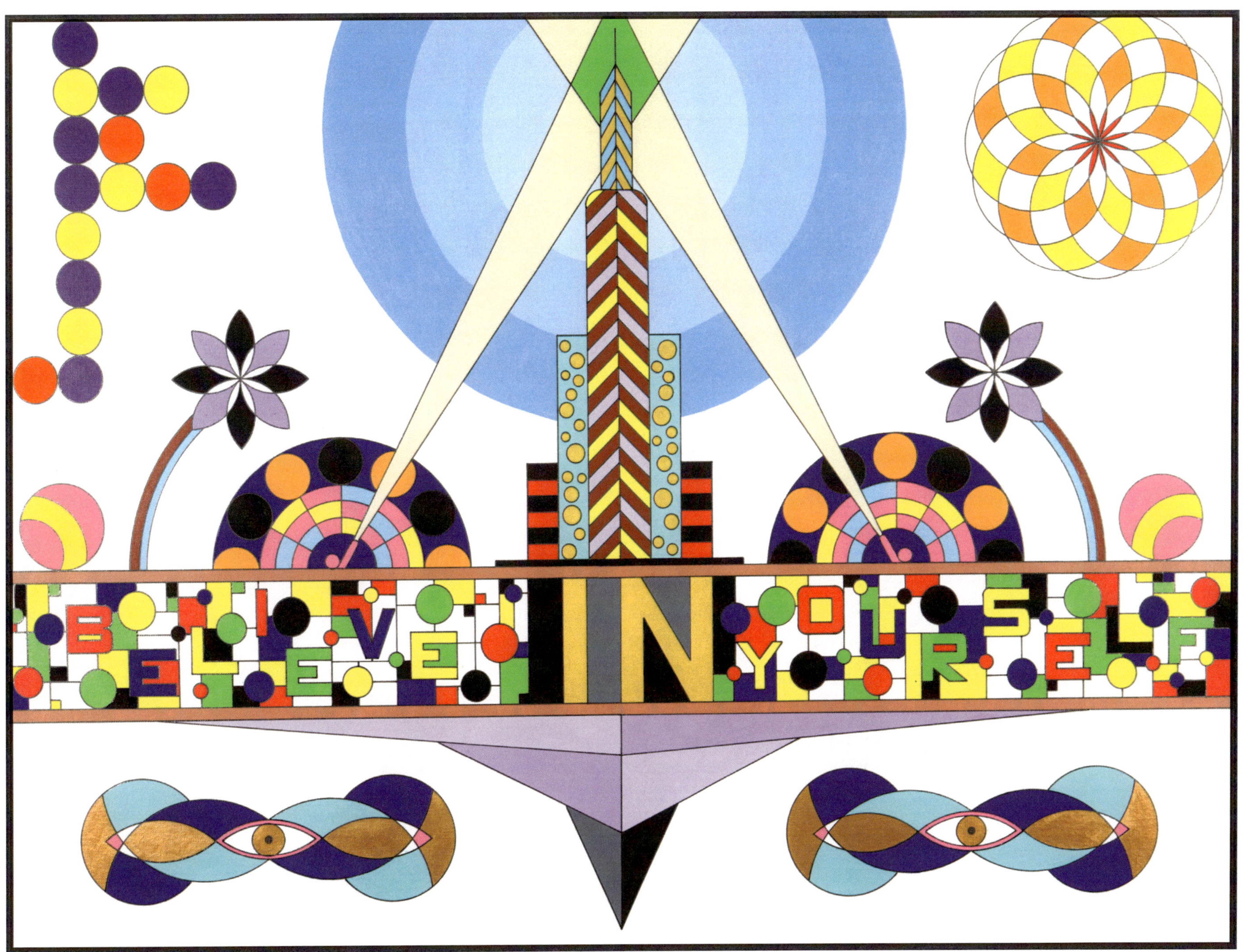

BELIEVE IN YOURSELF

'Preciate it Man!

36" x 48" Mixed media on canvas

"Gratitude is a powerful process for shifting your energy and bringing more of what you want into your life. Be grateful for what you already have, and you will attract more good things."
Rhonda Byrne

"Reflect upon your present blessings of which every man has many - not on your past misfortunes, of which all men have some."
Charles Dickens

"As we express our gratitude, we must never forget that the highest appreciation is not to utter words, but to live by them."
John F. Kennedy

"Gratitude unlocks the fullness of life. It turns what we have into enough, and more. It turns denial into acceptance, chaos to order, confusion to clarity. It can turn a meal into a feast, a house into a home, a stranger into a friend."
Melody Beattie

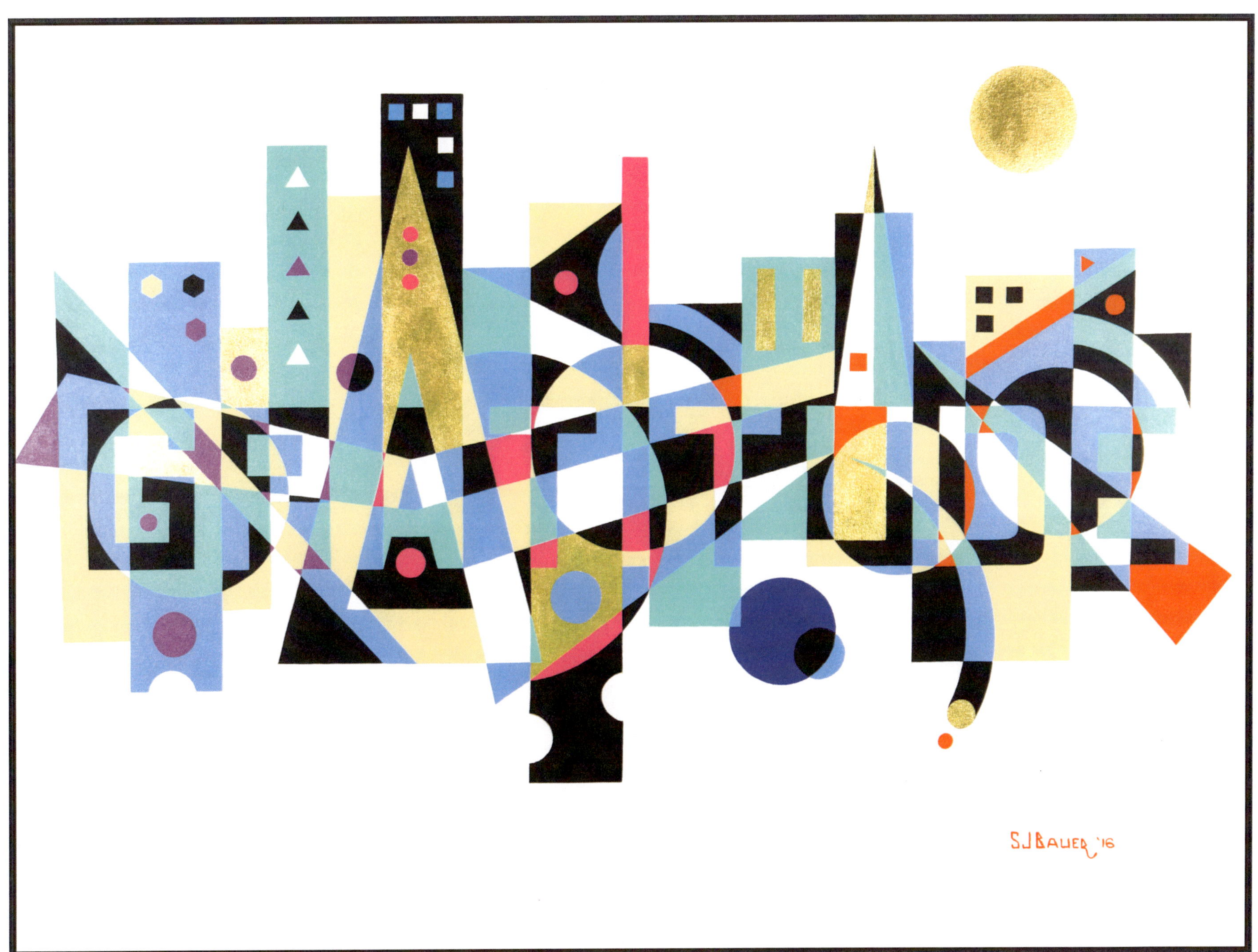

GRATITUDE
SJ BAUER '16

Like Peas and Carrots

36" x 48" Mixed media on canvas

"One must marry one's feelings to one's beliefs and ideas. That is probably the only way to achieve a measure of harmony in one's life."
Napoleon Hill

"The superior person is in harmony, but does not follow the crowd. The lesser person follows the crowd, but is not in harmony."
Confucius

"To our way of thinking the Indians' symbol is the circle, the hoop. Nature wants to be round. The bodies of human beings and animals have no corners. With us, the circle stands for togetherness of people who sit with one another around the campfire, relatives and friends united in peace while the sacred pipe passes from hand to hand. To us this is beautiful and fitting, symbol and reality at the same time, expressing the harmony of life and nature."
John Fire Lame Deer

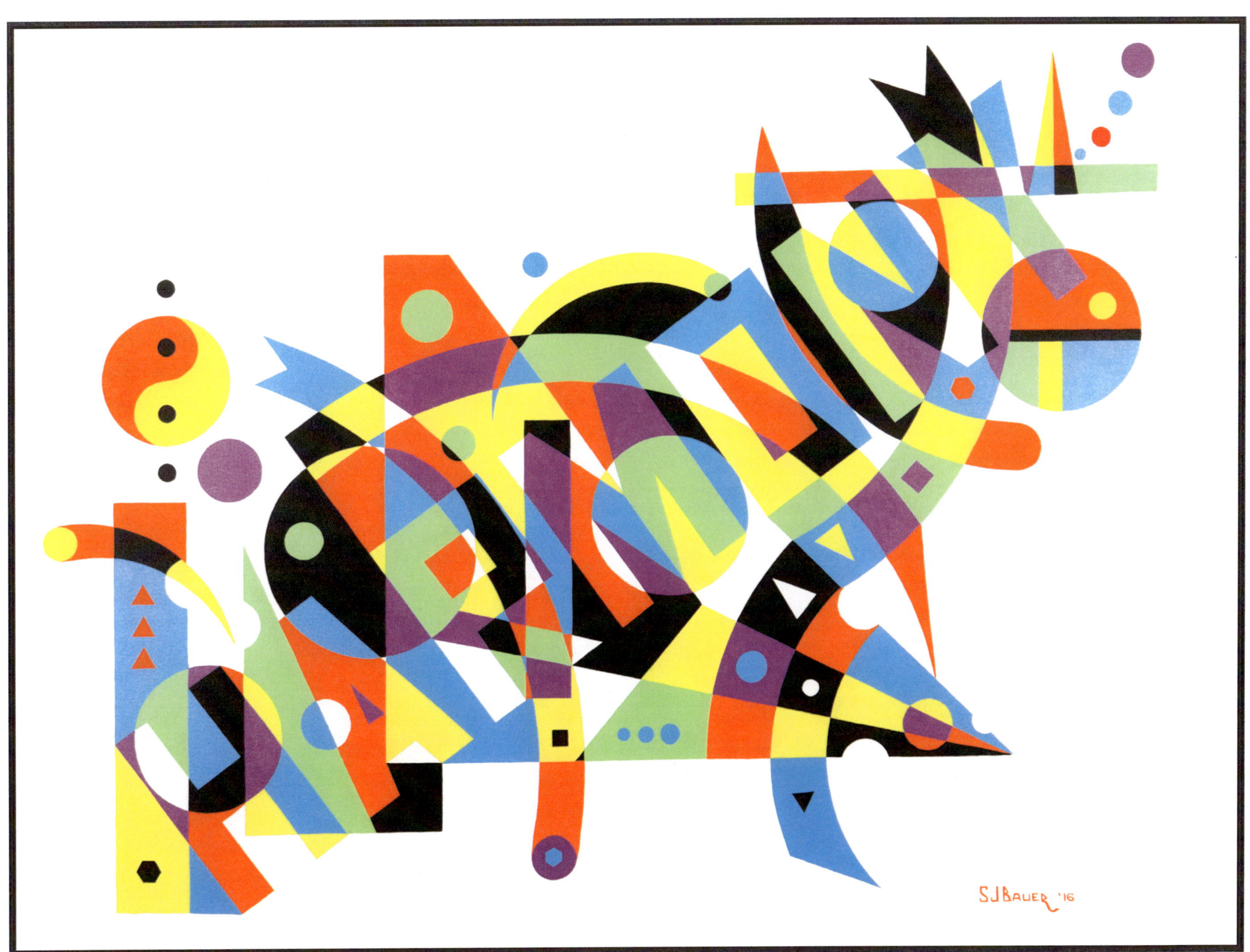
SJBauer '16

Fields of Grass, Forests of Green

48" x 48" Mixed media on canvas

"I feel the suffering of millions. And yet, when I look up at the sky, I somehow feel that every-thing will change for the better, that this cruelty too shall end, that peace and tranquility will return once more."
Anne Frank

"When you're at peace with your life and in a state of tranquility, you actually send out a vibration of energy that impacts all living creatures, including plants and animals."
Wayne Dyer

"In your occupations, try to possess your soul in peace. It is not a good plan to be in haste to perform any action that it may be the sooner over. On the contrary, you should accustom yourself to do whatever you have to do with tranquility, in order that you may retain the possession of yourself and of settled peace."
Jeanne Marie Bouvier de la Motte Guyon

"The more tranquil a man becomes, the greater is his success, his influence, his power for good. Calmness of mind is one of the beautiful jewels of wisdom."
James Allen

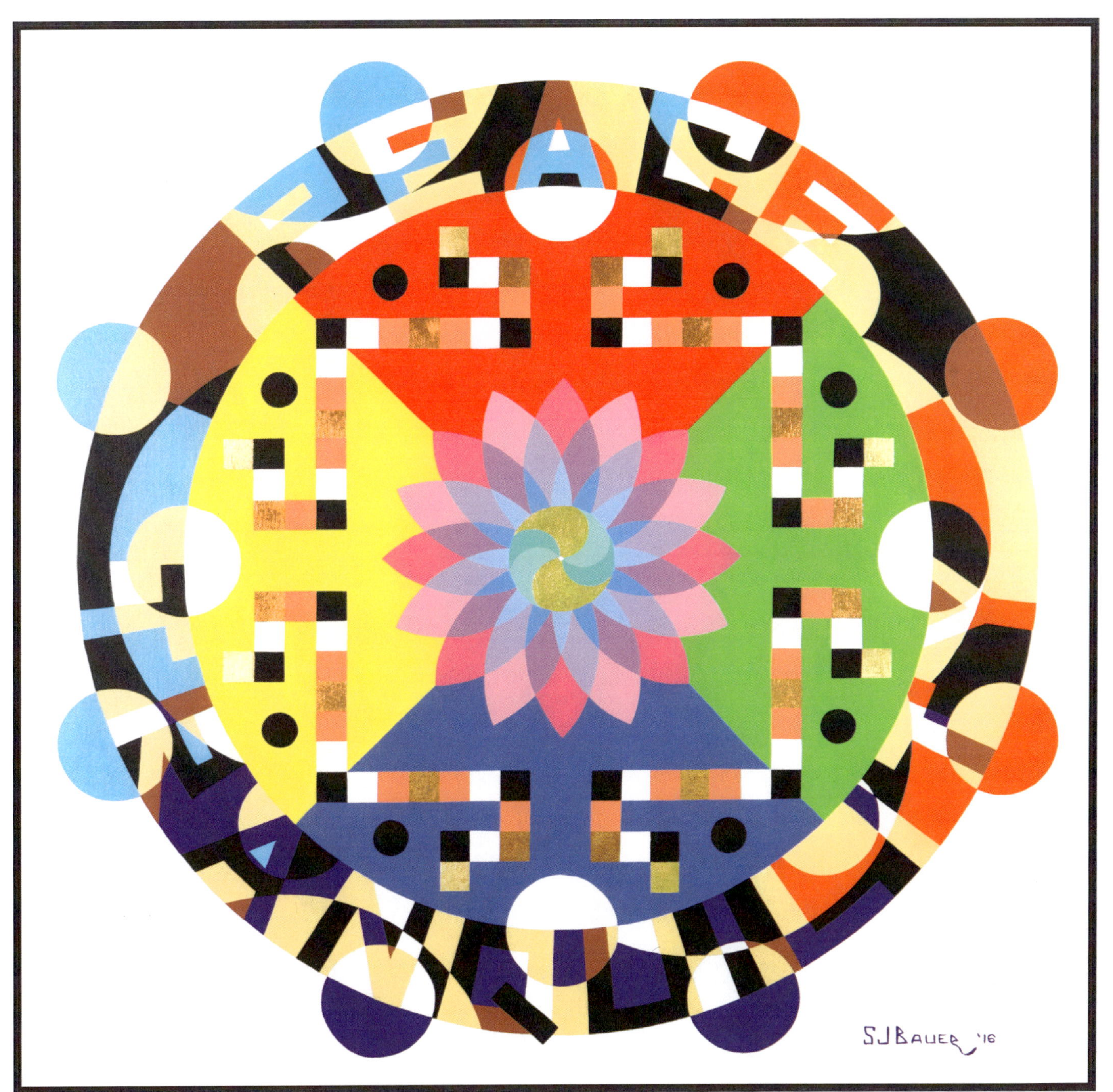
PEACE
SJBauer '16

Everythin's Ayrey

30" x 40" Acrylic on canvas

"Perhaps, after all, our best thoughts come when we are alone. It is good to listen, not to voices but to the wind blowing, to the brook running cool over polished stones, to bees drowsy with the weight of pollen. If we attend to the music of the earth, we reach serenity. And then, in some unexplained way, we share it with others."
Gladys Taber

"Curiosity endows the people who have it with a generosity in argument and a serenity in their own mode of life which springs from their cheerful willingness to let life take the form it will."
Alistair Cooke

"You can't calm the storm, so stop trying. What you can do is calm yourself. The storm will pass."
Timber Hawkeye

"Do your work, then step back. The only path to serenity."
Lao Tzu

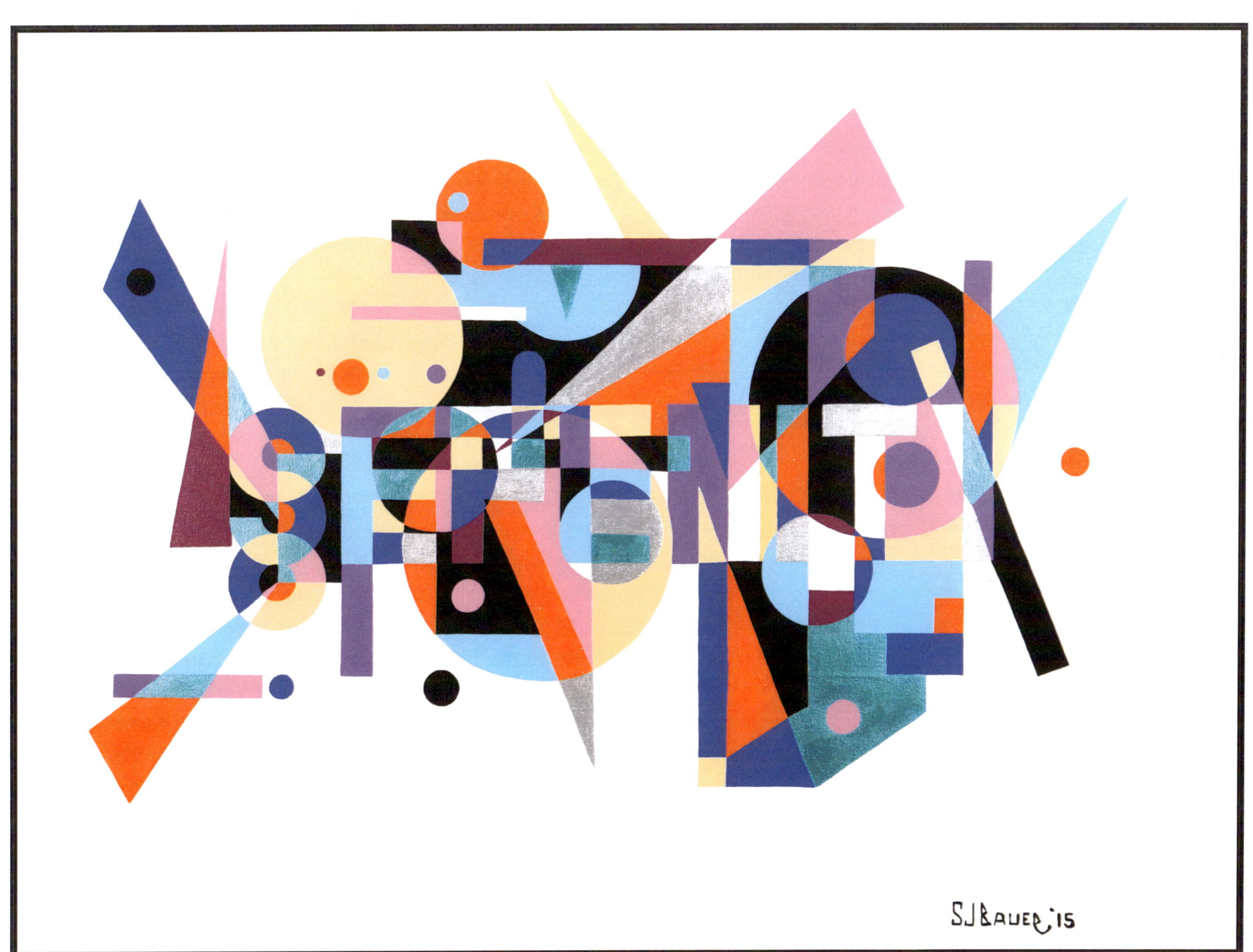

SJBauer '15

Livin' La Vida Loca

48" x 48" Acrylic on canvas

"Friendship is a sacred possession. As air, water and sunshine to flowers, trees and verdure, so smiles, sympathy and love of friends to the daily life of man. To live, laugh, love one's friends, and be loved by them is to bask in the sunshine of life."
David O. McKay

"The purpose of life is you smile, laugh as much as you breathe, and love as long as you live."
Eleanor Roosevelt

"This life is for loving, sharing, learning, smiling, caring, forgiving, laughing, hugging, helping, dancing, wondering, healing, and even more loving. I choose to live life this way. I want to live my life in such a way that when I get out of bed in the morning, the devil says, 'aw shit, he's up!'
Steve Maraboli

"Recipe for happiness: Live with enthusiasm, smile for no reason, love without conditions, act with purpose, listen with your heart, and laugh often."
Adrian Corday

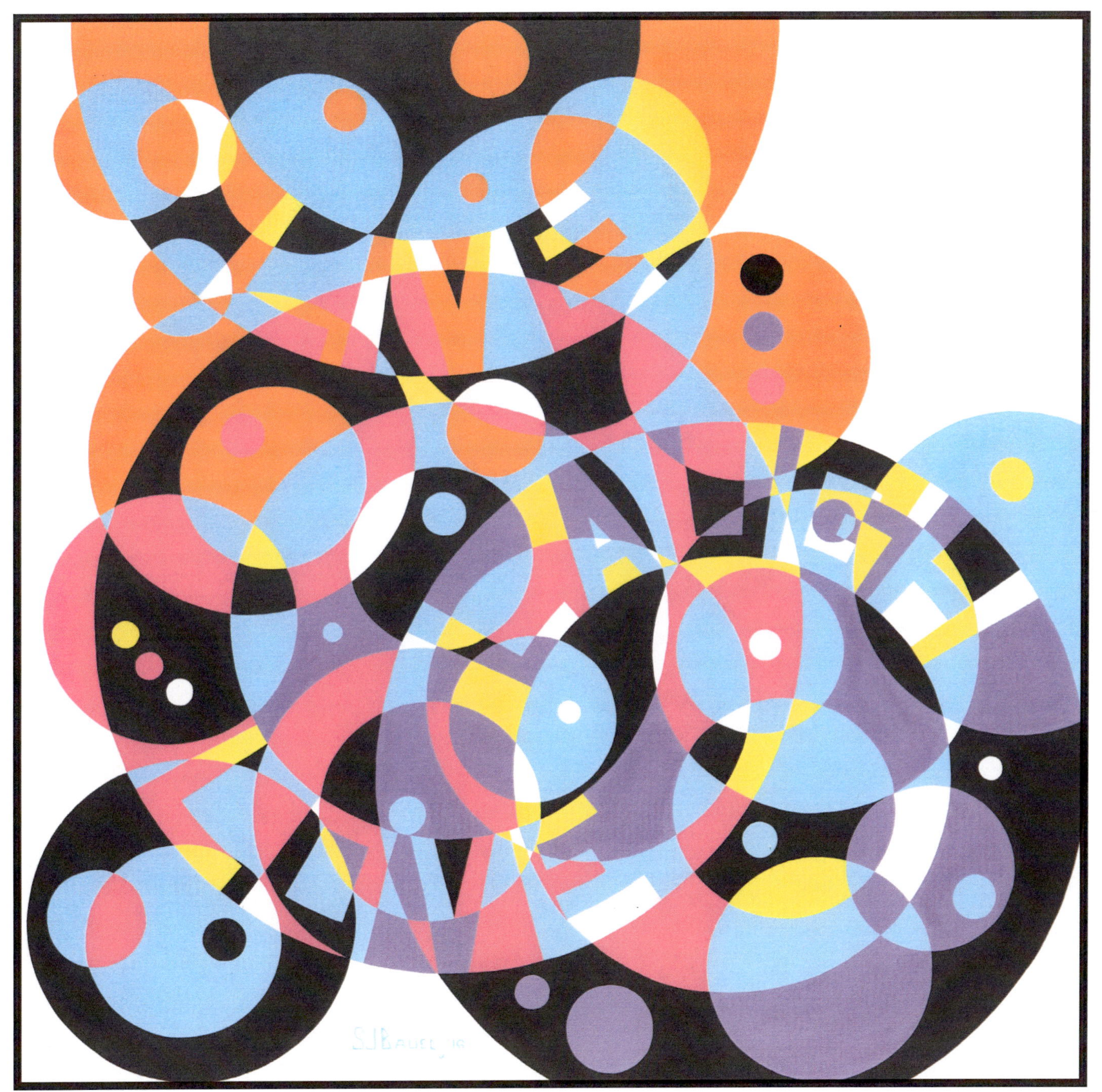

I Feel Ya

48" x 60" Acrylic on canvas

"The purpose of life is not to be happy. It is to be useful, to be honorable, to be compassionate, to have it make some difference that you have lived and lived well."
Ralph Waldo Emerson

"True compassion is more than flinging a coin to a beggar; it comes to see that an edifice which produces beggars needs restructuring."
Martin Luther King, Jr.

"I have just three things to teach: simplicity, patience, compassion. These three are your greatest treasures."
Lao Tzu

"Whether one believes in a religion or not, and whether one believes in rebirth or not, there isn't anyone who doesn't appreciate kindness and compassion."
Dalai Lama

"Compassion will cure more sins than condemnation."
Henry Ward Beecher

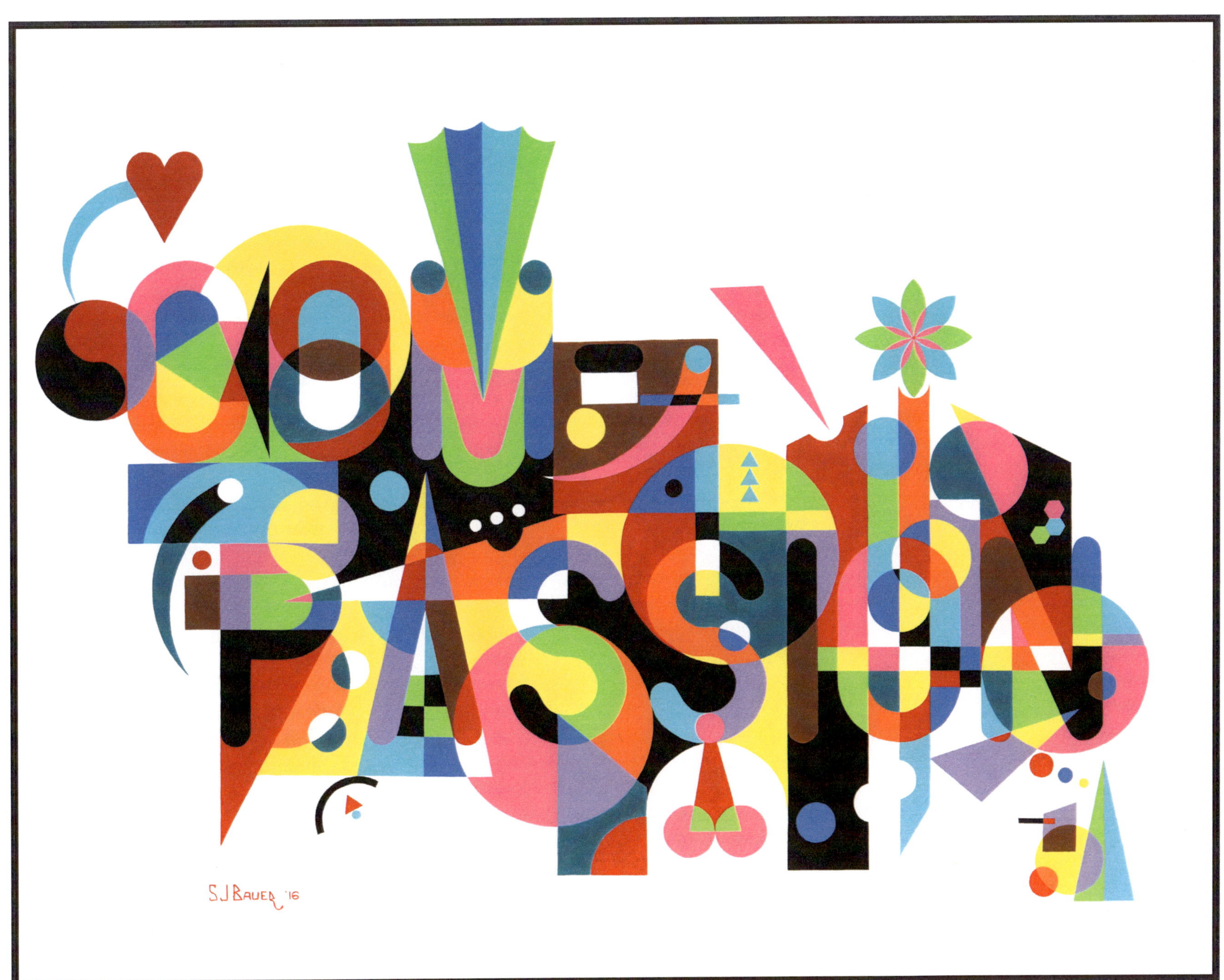

COMPASSION
SJ BAUER '16

Live and Let Live

48" x 48" Mixed media on canvas

"Tolerance implies no lack of commitment to one's own beliefs. Rather it condemns the oppression or persecution of others."
John F. Kennedy

"We need to promote greater tolerance and understanding among the peoples of the world. Nothing can be more dangerous to our efforts to build peace and development than a world divided along religious, ethnic or cultural lines. In each nation, and among all nations, we must work to promote unity based on our shared humanity."
Kofi Annan

"I learned that very often the most intolerant and narrow-minded people are the ones who congratulate themselves on their tolerance and open-mindedness."
Christopher Hitchens

"Sooner or later, if man is ever to be worthy of his destiny, we must fill our hearts with tolerance."
Stan Lee

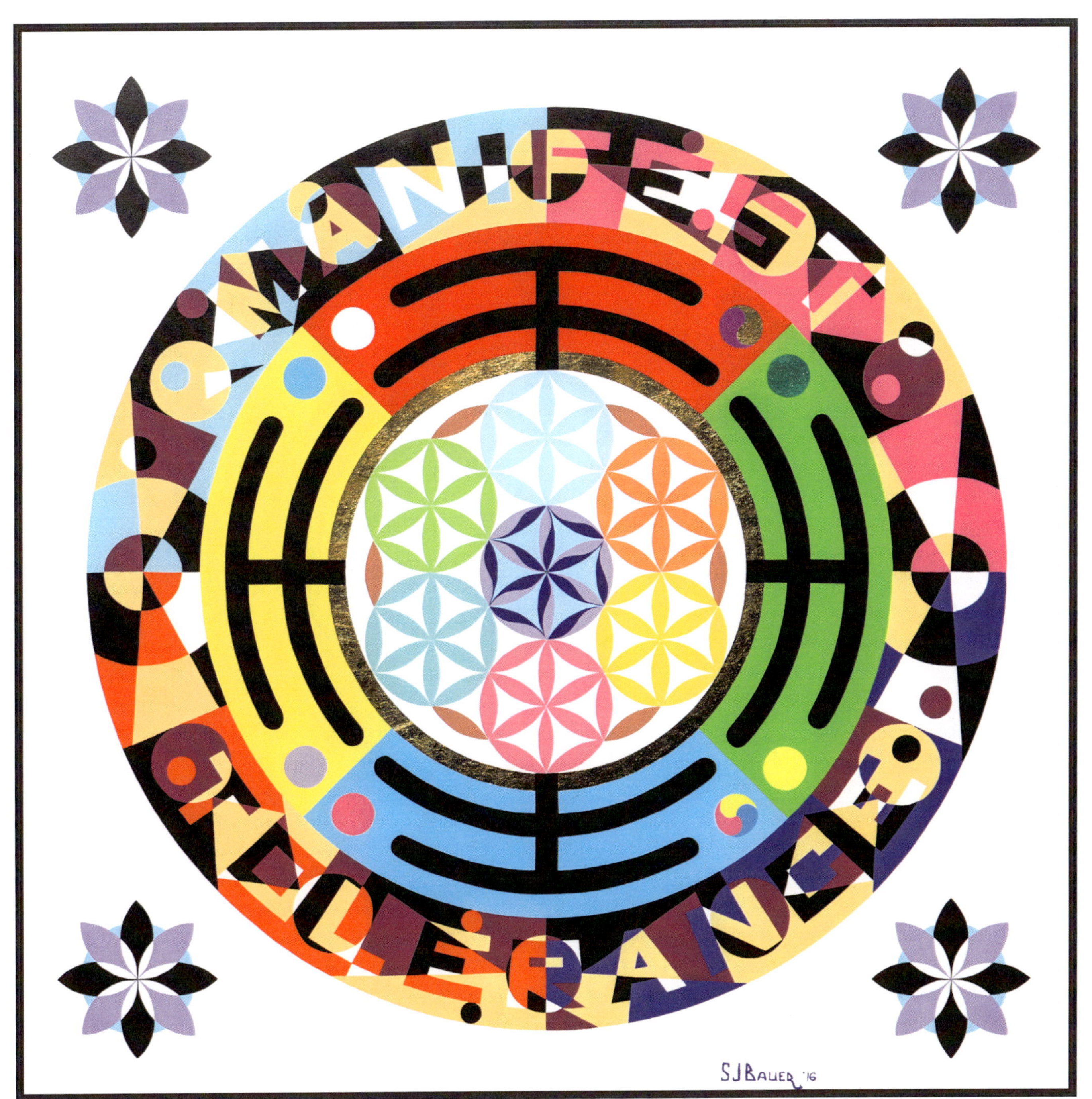

MANIFEST
TOLERANCE
SJBauer '16

I Really Mean It

24" x 48" Acrylic on canvas

"Sincerity is to speak as we think, to do as we pretend and profess, to perform and make good what we promise, and really to be what we would seem and appear to be."
John Tillotson

"I should say sincerity, a deep, great, genuine sincerity, is the first characteristic of all men in any way heroic."
Thomas Carlyle

"To practice five things under all circumstances constitutes perfect virtue; these five are gravity, generosity of soul, sincerity, earnestness, and kindness."
Confucius

"When you really need help, people will respond. Sincerity means dropping the image facade and showing a willingness to be vulnerable. Tell it the way it is, lumps and all. Don't worry if your presentation isn't perfect; ask from your heart. Keep it simple, and people will open up to you."
Jack Canfield

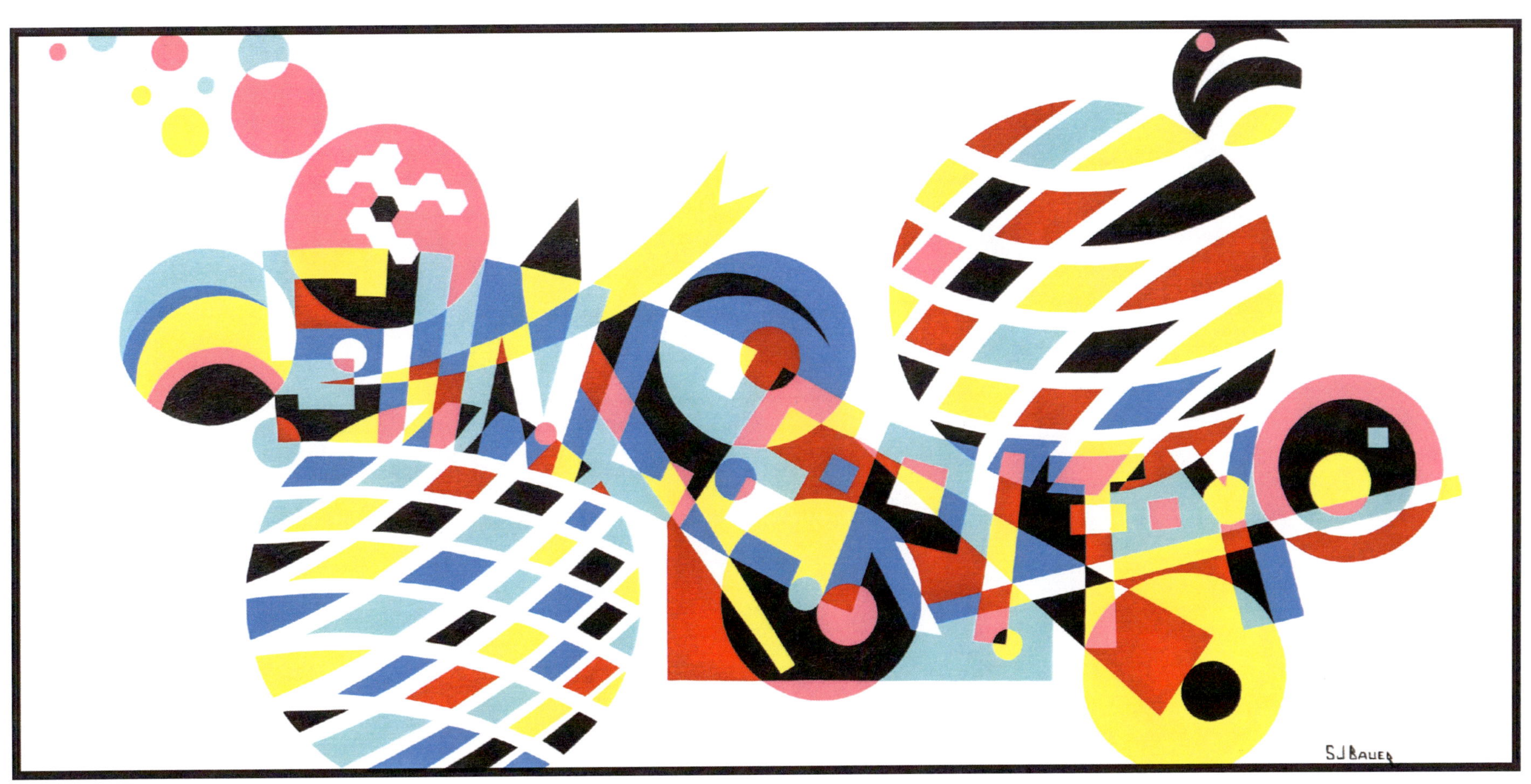

SJ BAUER

Springs Eternal

24" x 24" Mixed media on canvas

"Hope has two beautiful daughters; their names are Anger and Courage. Anger at the way things are, and Courage to see that they do not remain as they are."
Saint Augustine

"Most of the important things in the world have been accomplished by people who have kept on trying when there seemed to be no hope at all."
Dale Carnegie

"Be careful to leave your sons well instructed rather than rich, for the hopes of the instructed are better than the wealth of the ignorant."
Epictetus

"Hope is important because it can make the present moment less difficult to bear. If we believe that tomorrow will be better, we can bear a hardship today."
Thich Nhat Hanh

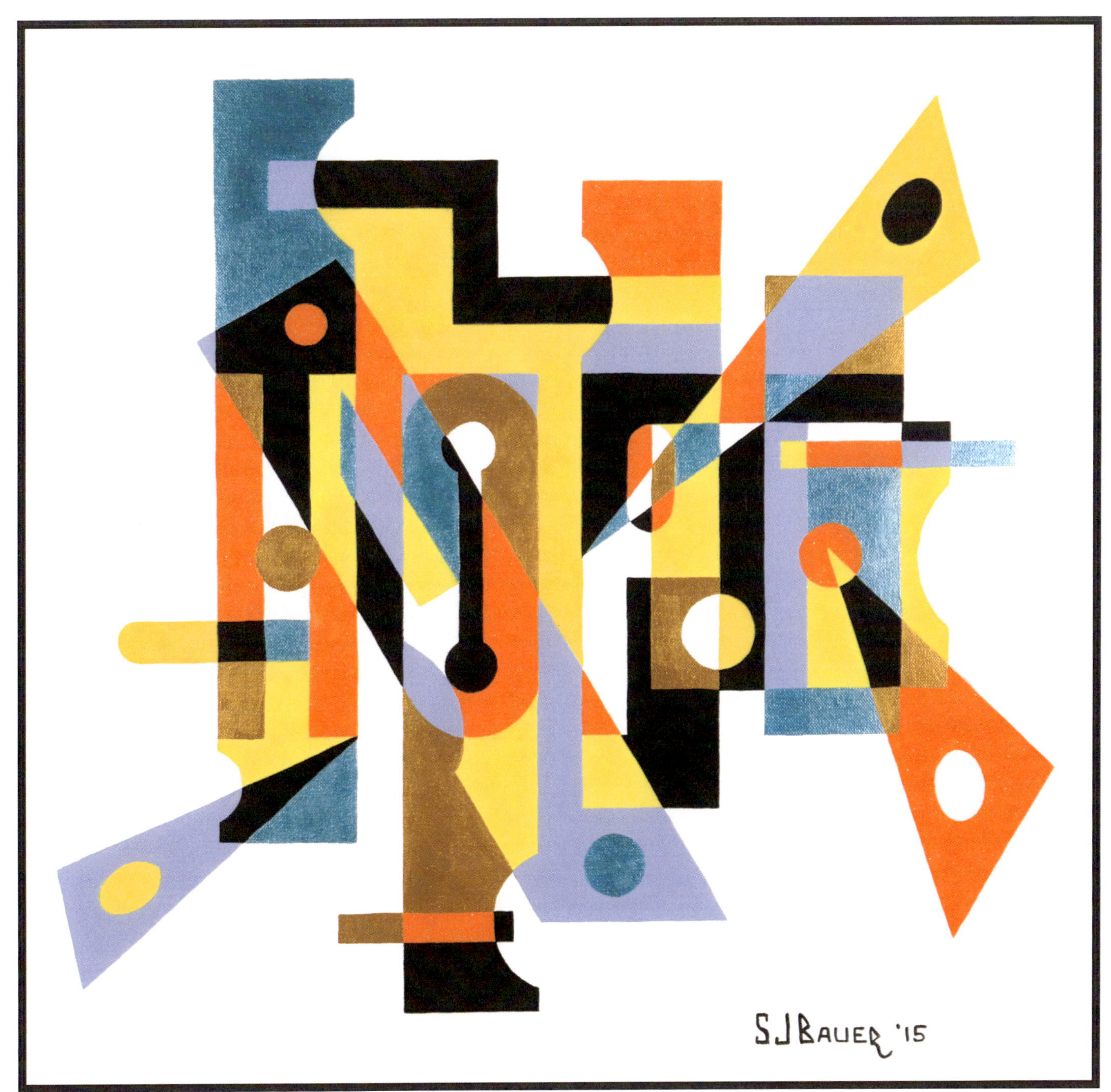

SJ Bauer '15

We Are All The Same

36" x 36" Acrylic on canvas

"I think that we must face the fact that in reality, you cannot have economic and political equality without having some form of social equality. I think this is inevitable."
Martin Luther King, Jr.

"At a time when efforts are being made to eradicate discrimination between the sexes in the search for social equality and justice, the differences between the sexes are being rediscovered."
Carol Gilligan

"In America everybody is of the opinion that he has no social superiors, since all men are equal, but he does not admit that he has no social inferiors, for, from the time of Jefferson onward, the doctrine that all men are equal applies only upwards, not downwards."
Bertrand Russell

"Democracy and socialism have nothing in common but one word, equality. But notice the difference: while democracy seeks equality in liberty, socialism seeks equality in restraint and servitude."
Alexis de Tocqueville

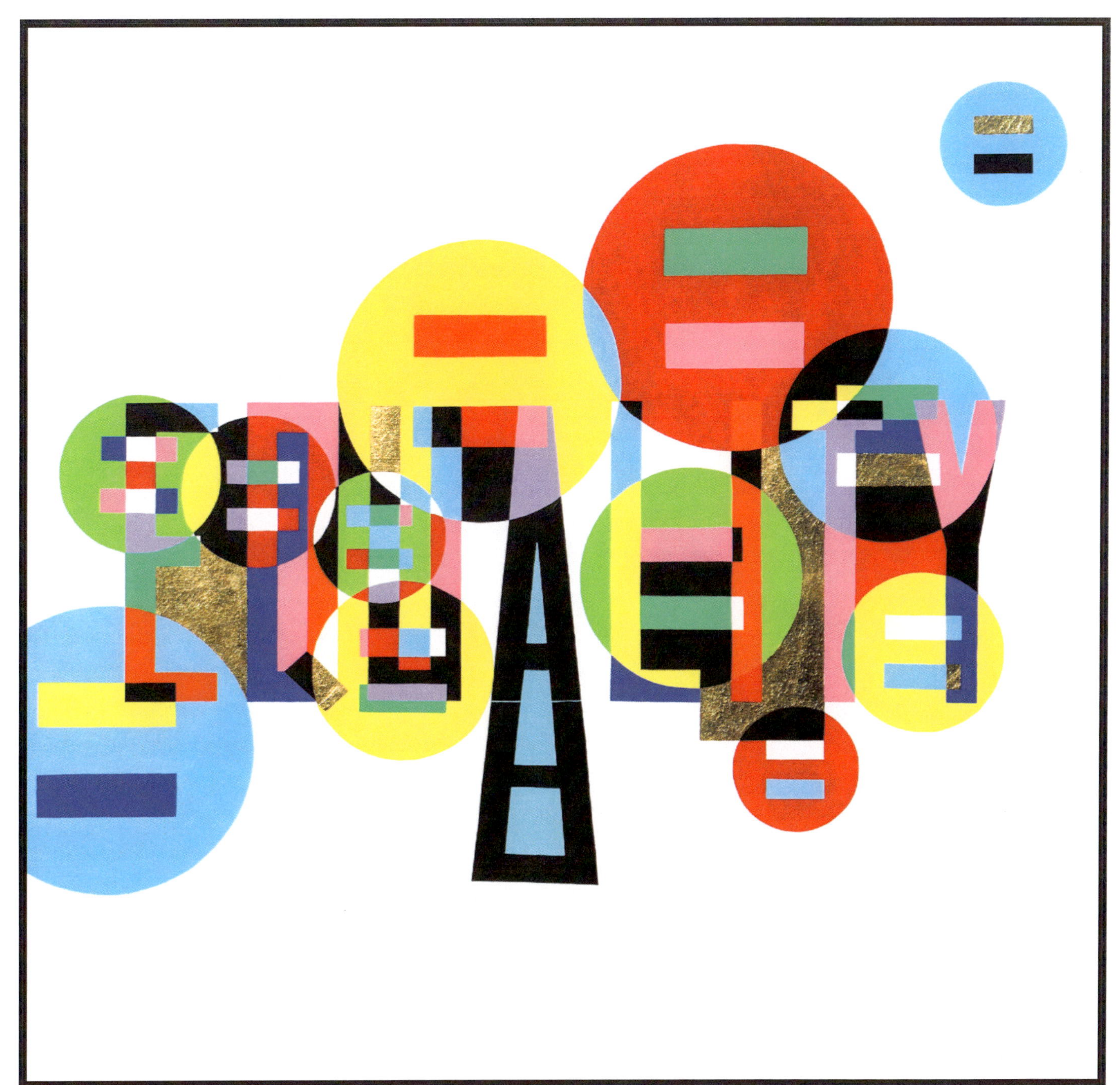

Key to the Universe

18" x 24" Mixed media on canvas

"Don't limit yourself. Many people limit themselves to what they think they can do. You can go as far as your mind lets you. What you believe, remember, you can achieve."
Mary Kay Ash

"Man often becomes what he believes himself to be. If I keep on saying to myself that I cannot do a certain thing, it is possible that I may end by really becoming incapable of doing it. On the contrary, if I have the belief that I can do it, I shall surely acquire the capacity to do it even if I may not have it at the beginning."
Mahatma Gandhi

"If you want to be successful, it's just this simple. Know what you are doing. Love what you are doing. And believe in what you are doing."
Will Rogers

"Once we believe in ourselves, we can risk curiosity, wonder, spontaneous delight, or any experience that reveals the human spirit."
e. e. cummings

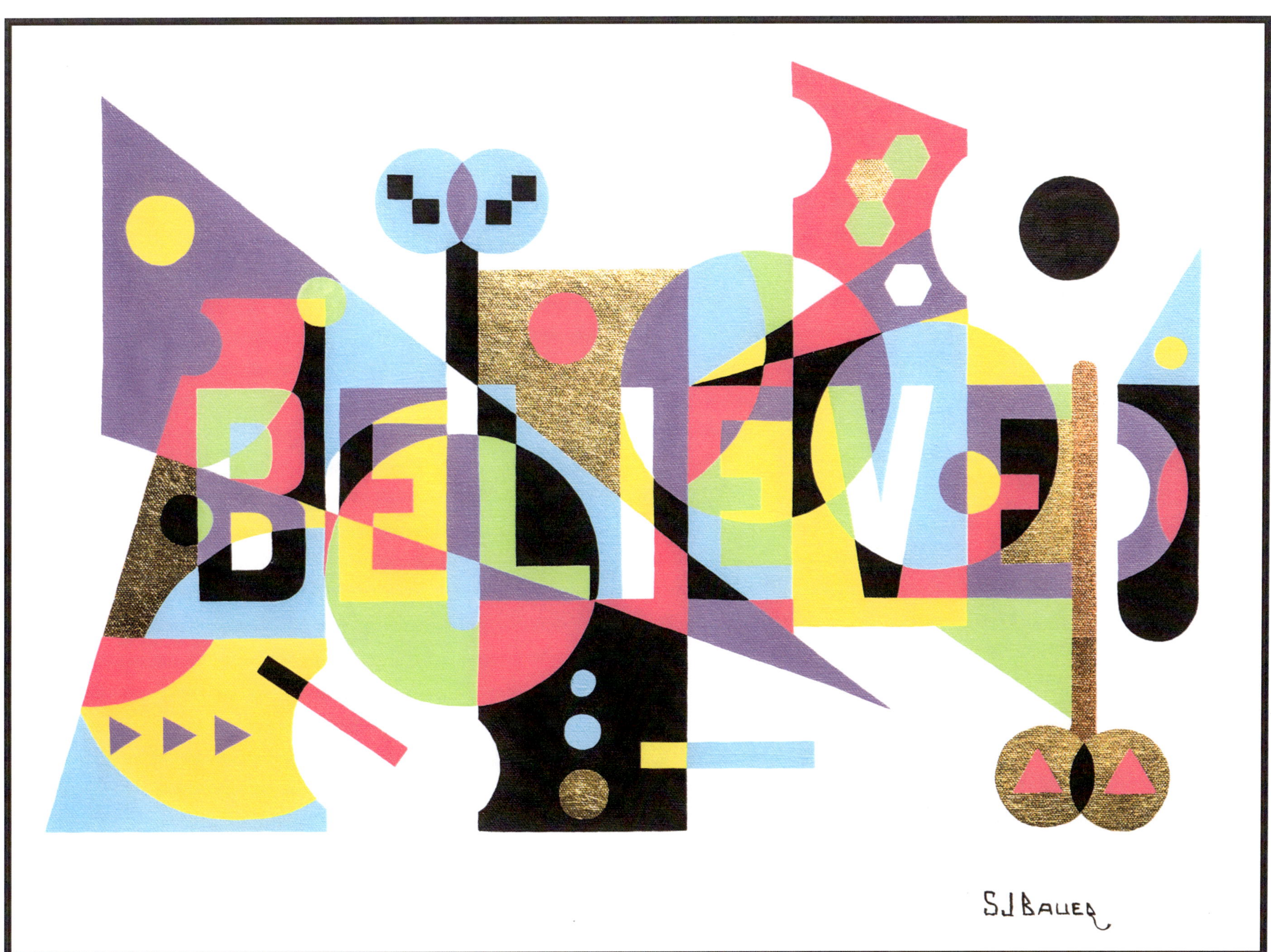
BELIEVE
SJ Bauer

You Are Better Than This

48" x 48" Acrylic on canvas

"Little minds are tamed and subdued by misfortune; but great minds rise above them."
Washington Irving

"To succeed, it is necessary to accept the world as it is and rise above it."
Michael Korda

"You ought to know how to rise above the trivialities of life, in which most people are found drowning themselves."
D.T. Suzuki

"Life isn't fair. It's true, and you still have to deal with it. Whining about it rarely levels the playing field, but learning to rise above it is the ultimate reward."
Harvey Mackay

"As leaders, we need to rise above petty politics and lead, rather than follow, the various interests and pressure groups in our respective countries."
Hassan Rouhani

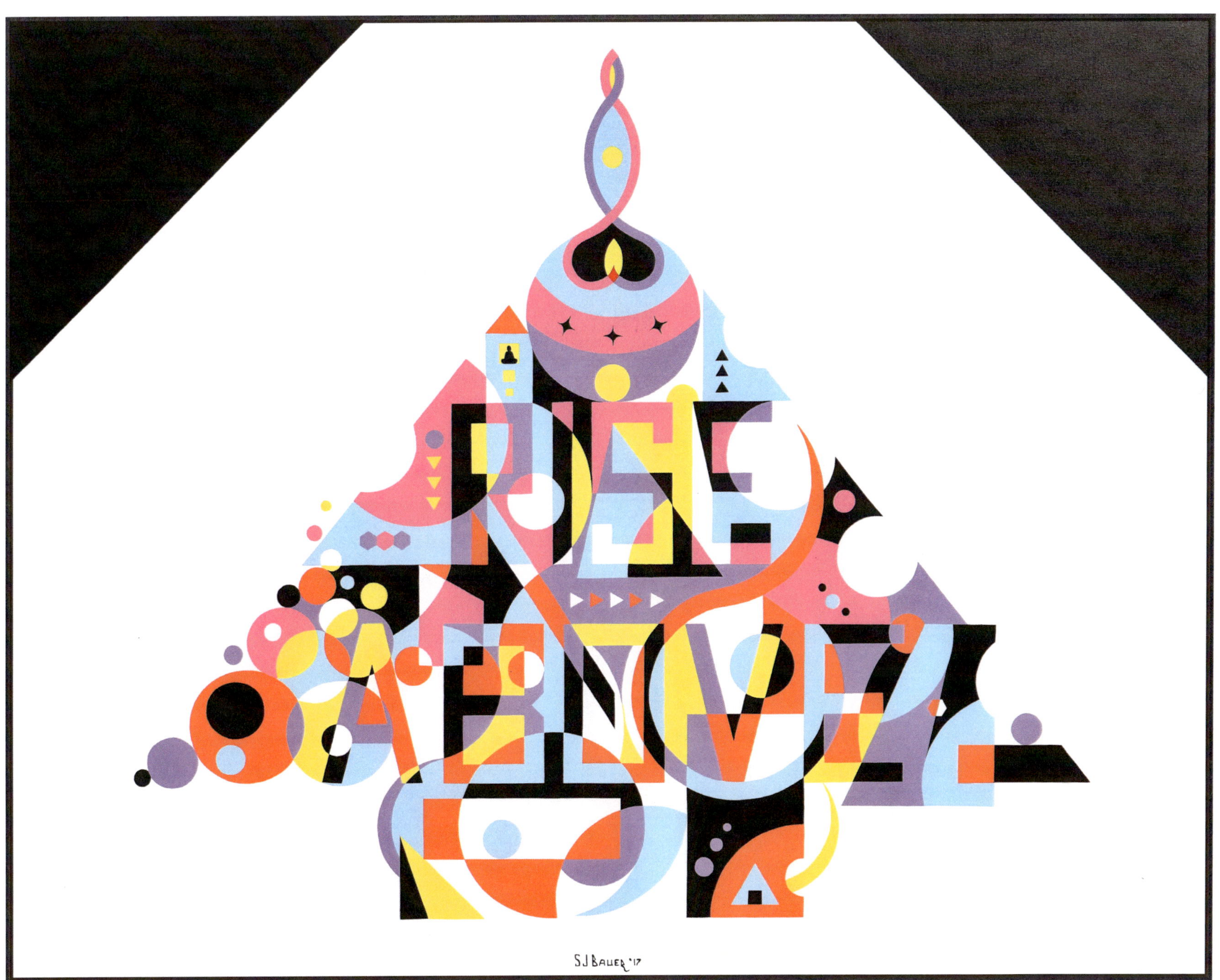

RISE
ABOVE
IT
SJ BAUER '17

What Goes Around

30" x 48" Acrylic on canvas

"Kindness is the language which the deaf can hear and the blind can see."
Mark Twain

"No act of kindness, no matter how small, is ever wasted."
Aesop

"Be kind, for everyone you meet is fighting a battle you know nothing about."
Wendy Mass

"Whatever possession we gain by our sword cannot be sure or lasting, but the love gained by kindness and moderation is certain and durable."
Alexander the Great

"Constant kindness can accomplish much. As the sun makes ice melt, kindness causes misunderstanding, mistrust, and hostility to evaporate."
Albert Schweitzer

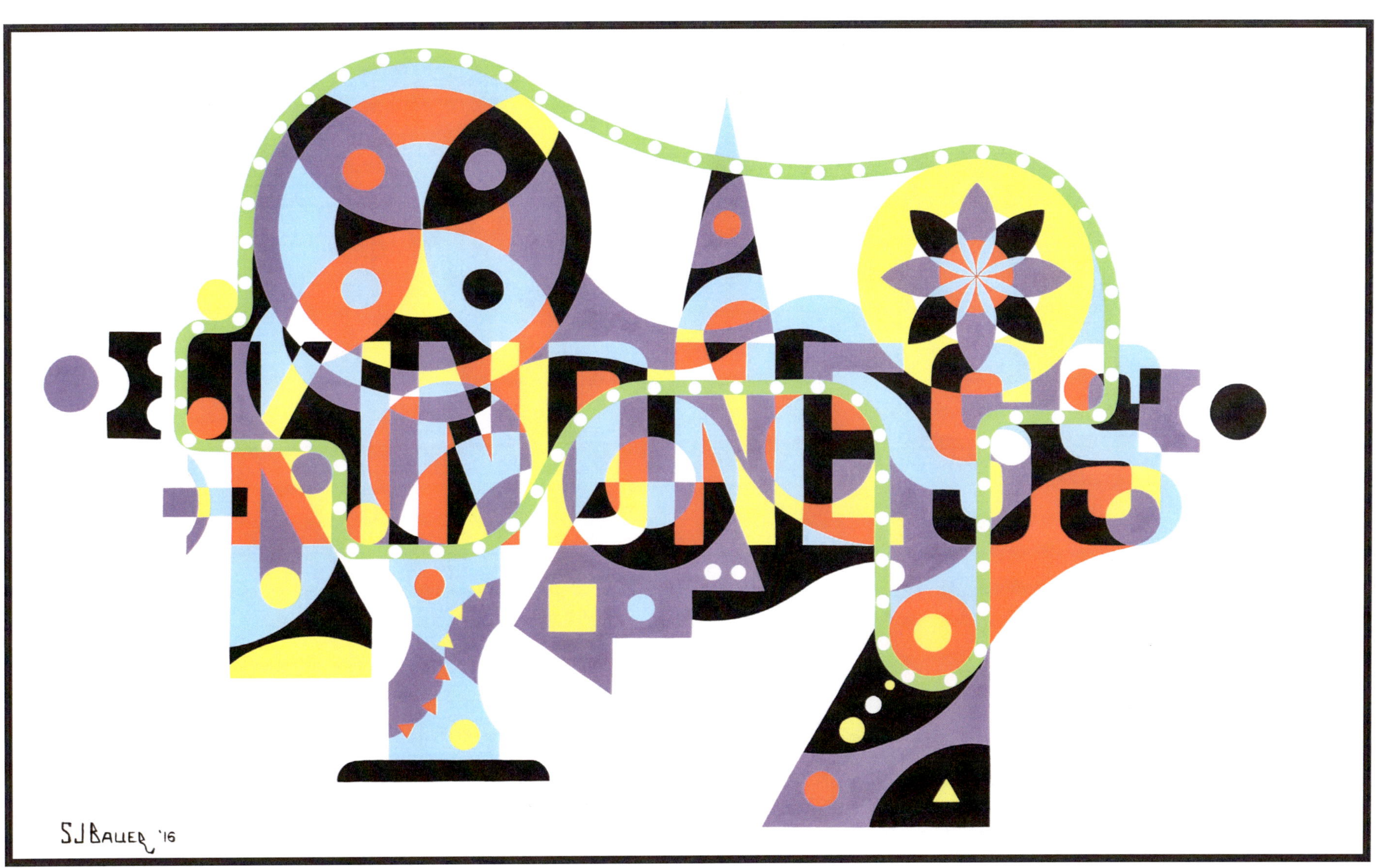

Give 'Til it Hurts

36" x 48" Acrylic on canvas

"No one has ever become poor by giving."
Anne Frank

"You have not lived today until you have done something for someone who can never repay you."
John Bunyan

"Generosity is not giving me that which I need more than you do, but it is giving me that which you need more than I do."
Khalil Gibran

"Virtues, like viruses, have their seasons of contagion. When catastrophe strikes, generosity spikes like a fever. Courage spreads in the face of tyranny."
Nancy Gibbs

"Generosity during life is a very different thing from generosity in the hour of death; one proceeds from genuine liberality and benevolence, the other from pride or fear."
Horace Mann

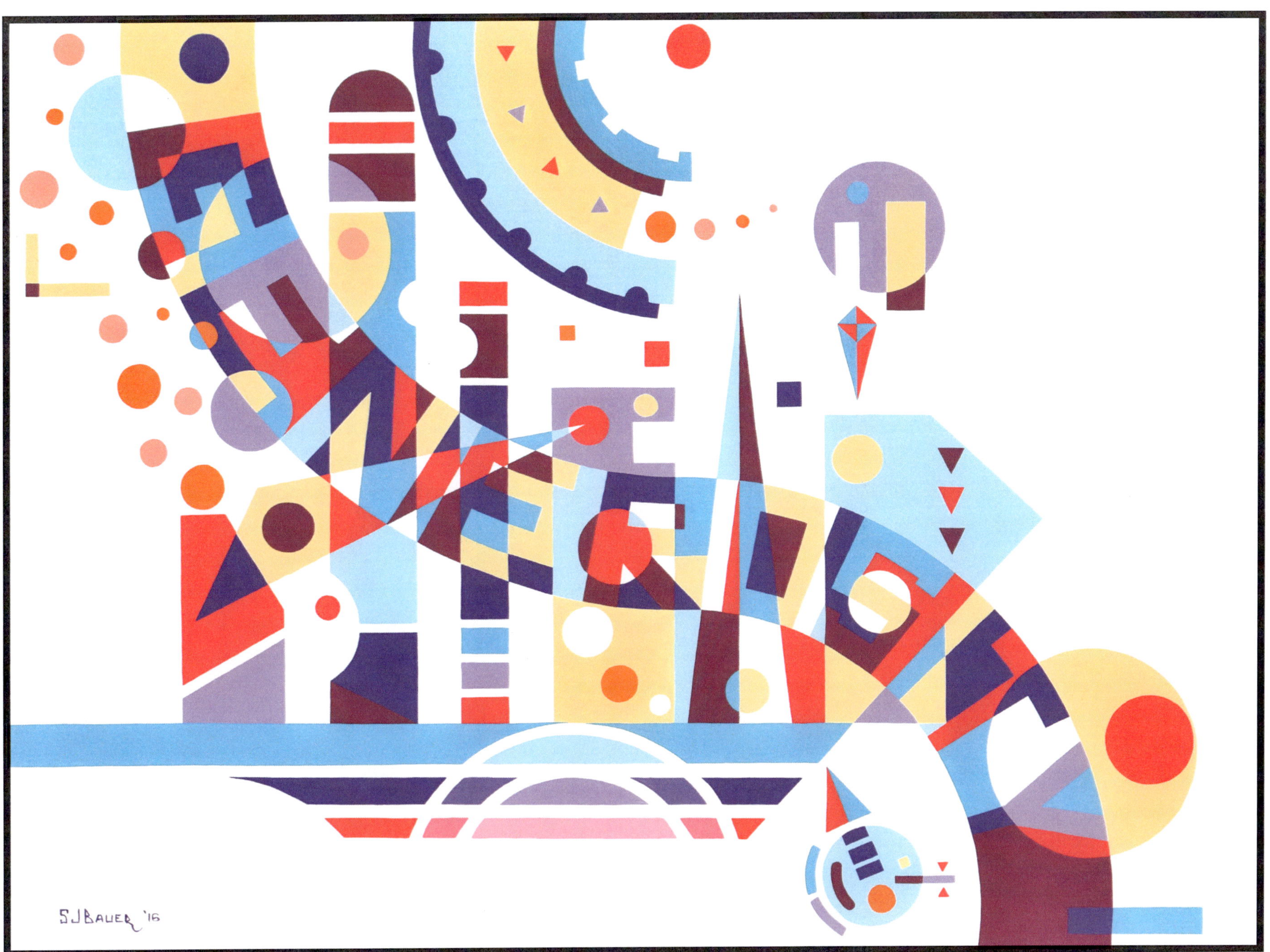

SJBauer '16

It's All You Need

24" x 24" Mixed media on canvas

"To love someone is nothing, to be loved by someone is something, to love someone who loves you is everything."
Bill Russell

"Sometimes people put up walls, not to keep others out, but to see who cares enough to break them down."
Banana Yoshimoto

"I love you not only for what you are, but for what I am when I am with you"
Roy Croft

"Love is like a beautiful flower which I may not touch, but whose fragrance makes the garden a place of delight just the same."
Helen Keller

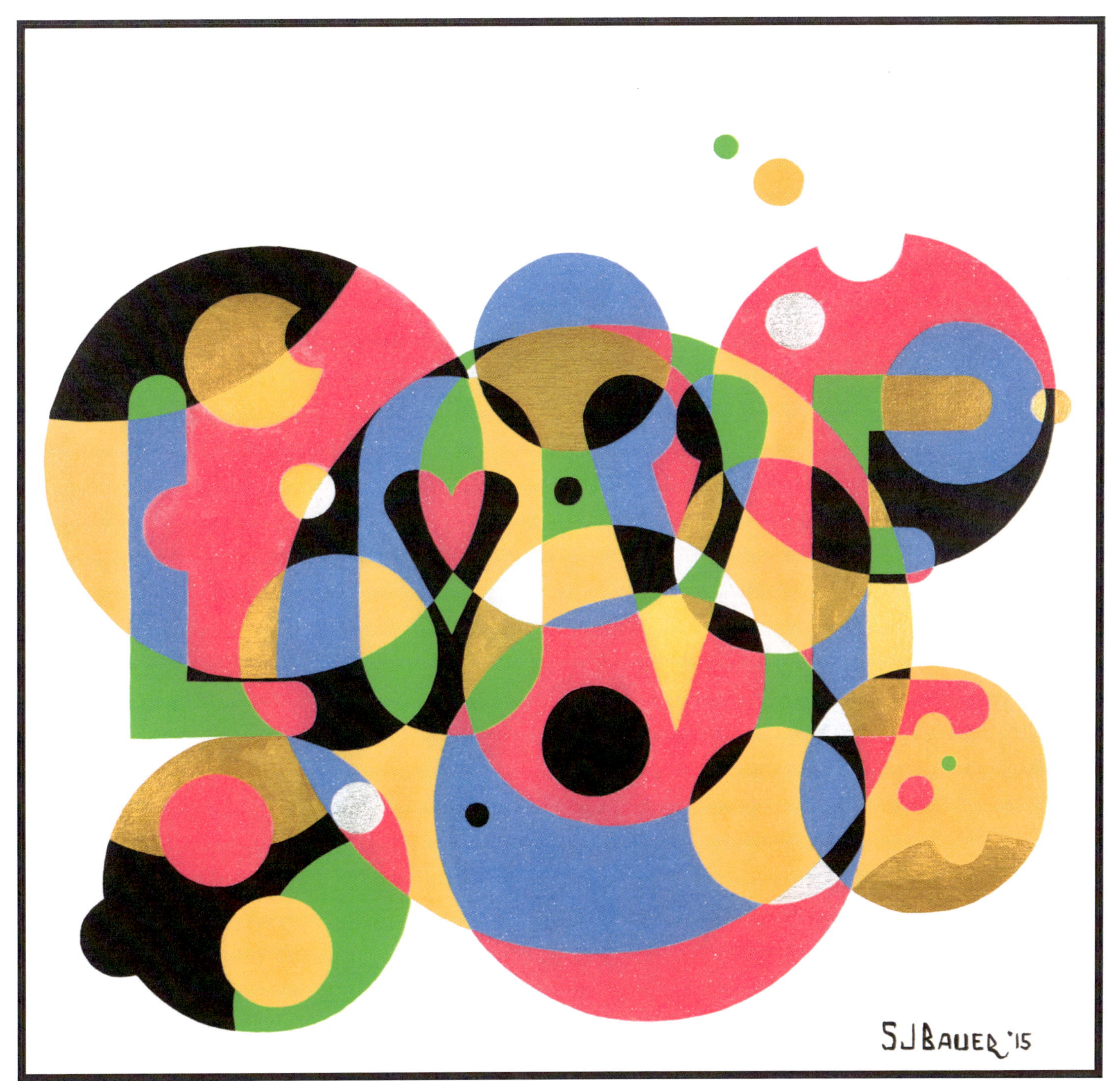
SJBauer '15

Sock it to Me

18" x 24" Acrylic on canvas

"One of the most sincere forms of respect is actually listening to what another has to say."
Bryant H. McGill

"The American ideal is not that we all agree with each other, or even like each other, every minute of the day. It is rather that we will respect each other's rights, especially the right to be different, and that, at the end of the day, we will understand that we are one people, one country, and one community, and that our well-being is inextricably bound up with the well-being of each and every one of our fellow citizens."
C. Everett Koop

"When you are content to be simply yourself and don't compare or compete, everyone will respect you."
Lao Tzu

"To be one, to be united is a great thing. But to respect the right to be different is maybe even greater."
Bono

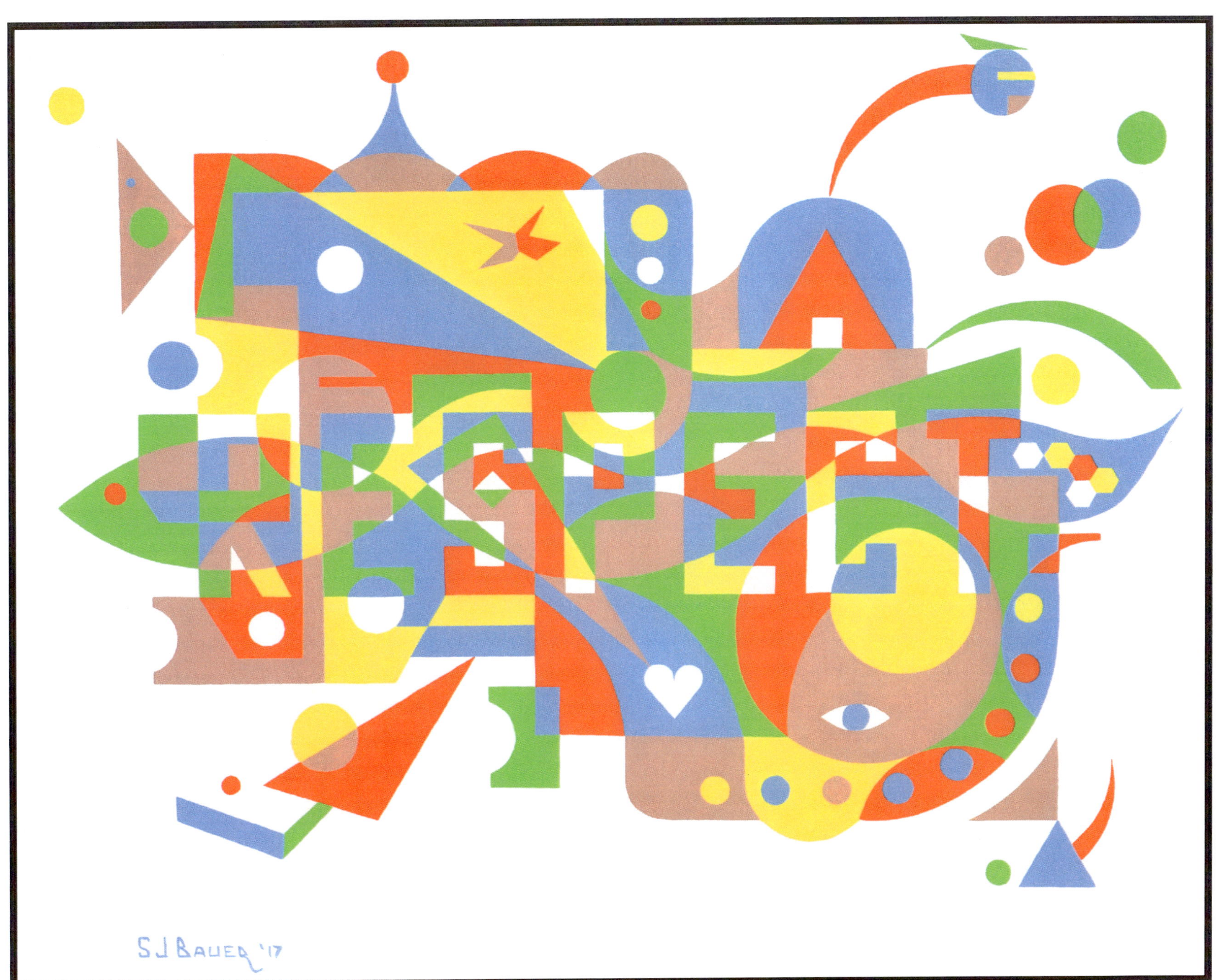

RESPECT
SJ BAUER '17

We're Stronger Together

48" x 60" Acrylic on canvas

"United we stand, divided we fall. Let us not split into factions which must destroy that union upon which our existence hangs."
Patrick Henry

"We must learn to live together as brothers or perish together as fools."
Martin Luther King, Jr.

"The essence of America — that which really unites us — is not ethnicity, or nationality or religion — it is an idea — and what an idea it is: That you can come from humble circumstances and do great things."
Condoleezza Rice

"This country will not be a good place for any of us to live in unless we make it a good place for all of us to live in."
Theodore Roosevelt

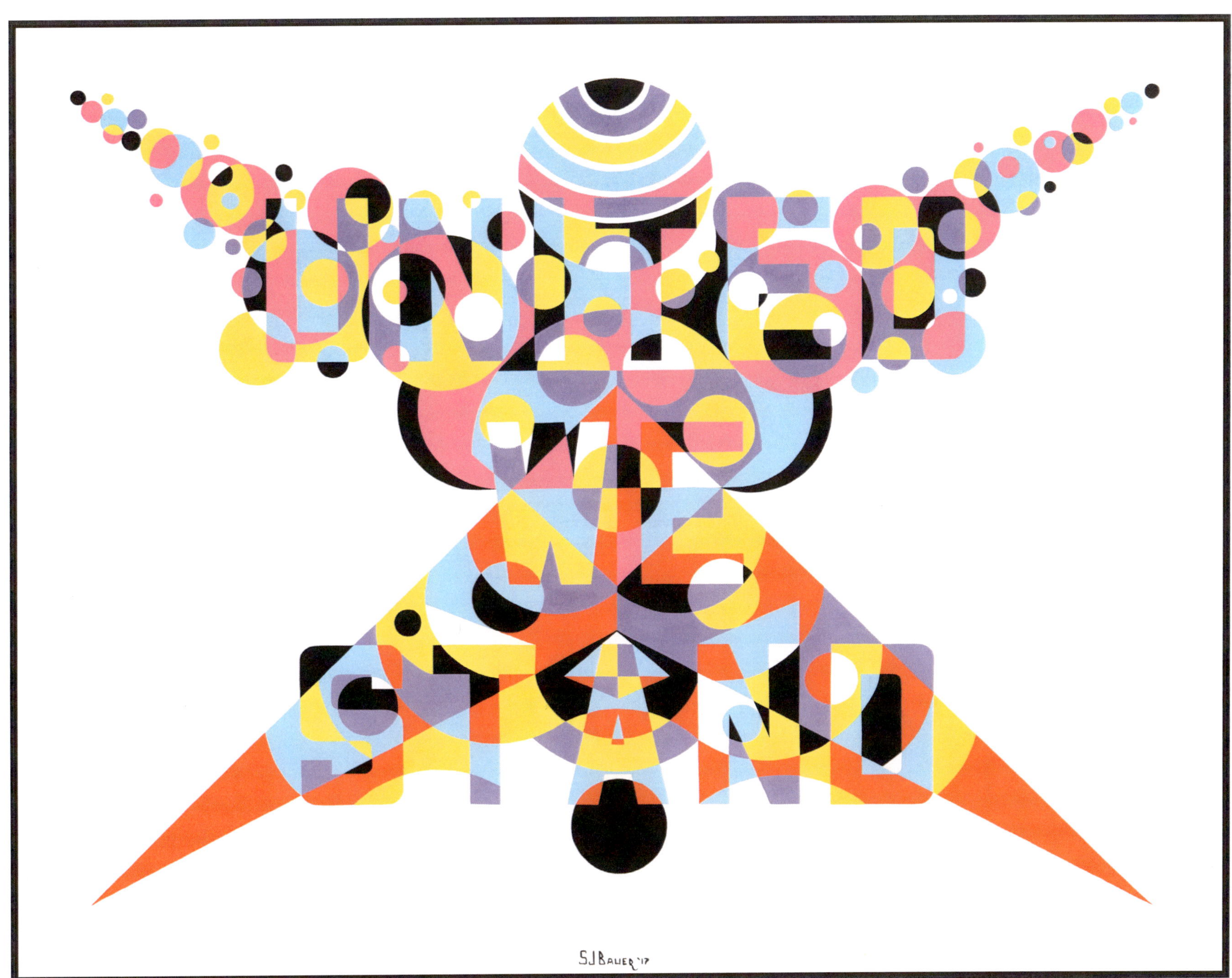

UNITED
WE
STAND
SJ BAUER '17

Lead by Example

30" x 30" Acrylic on canvas

"If your actions inspire others to dream more, learn more, do more and become more, you are a leader."
John Quincy Adams

"I've learned that people will forget what you said, people will forget what you did, but people will never forget how you made them feel."
Maya Angelou

"A word of encouragement from a teacher to a child can change a life. A word of encouragement from a spouse can save a marriage. A word of encouragement from a leader can inspire a person to reach her potential."
John C. Maxwell

"Civil disobedience's main goal typically is to try to arouse and inspire others to join and do something. Well, sometimes that is a good tactic, sometimes not."
Noam Chomsky

____

____

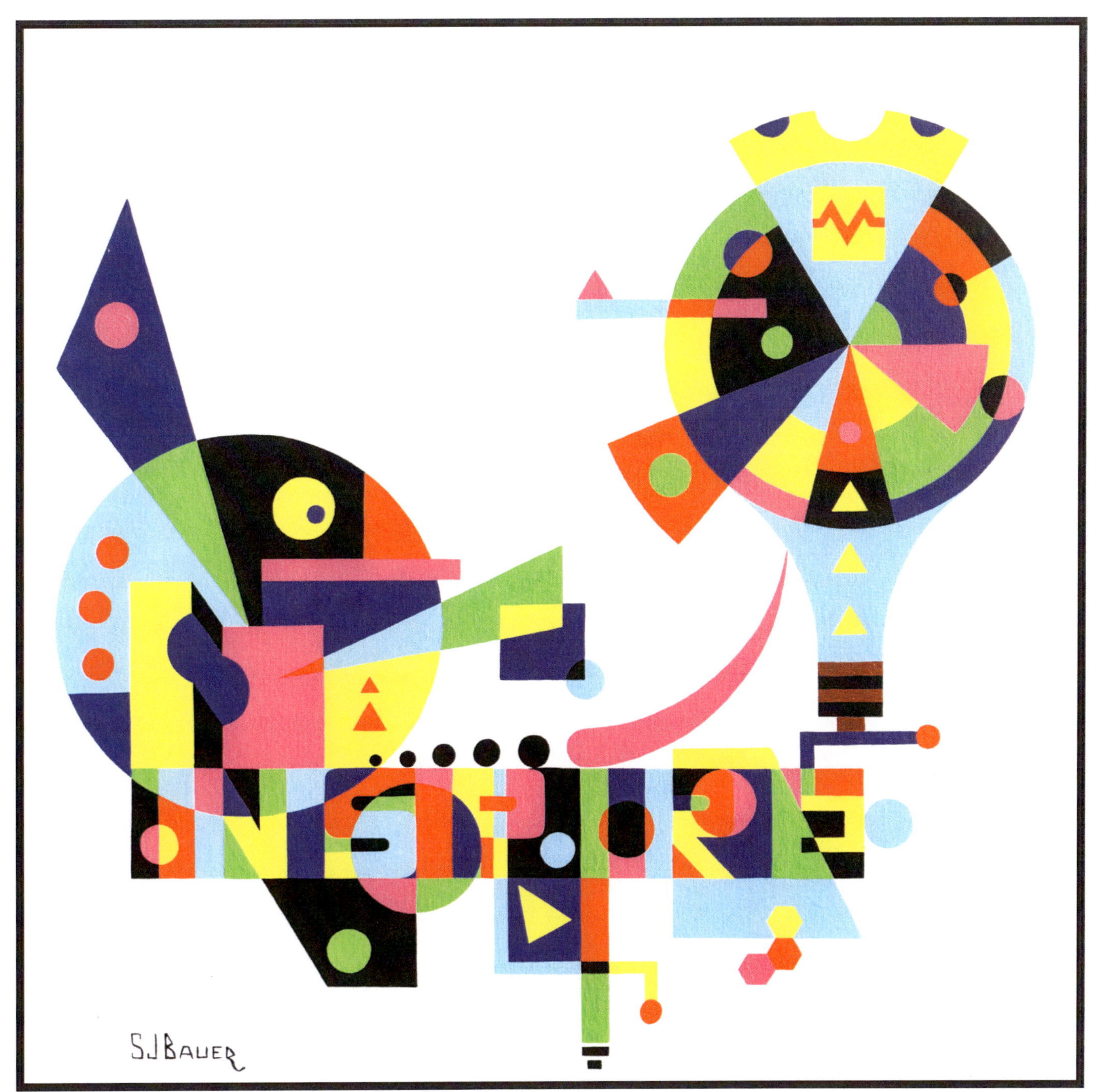

INSPIRE
SJBAUER

I Don't Need Proof

24" x 24" Mixed media on canvas

"Faith sees the invisible, believes the unbelievable, and receives the impossible."
Corrie Ten Boom

"Faith is the first factor in a life devoted to service. Without it, nothing is possible. With it, nothing is impossible."
Mary McLeod Bethune

"The faith that stands on authority is not faith."
Ralph Waldo Emerson

"God... a being whose only definition is that he is beyond man's power to conceive."
Ayn Rand

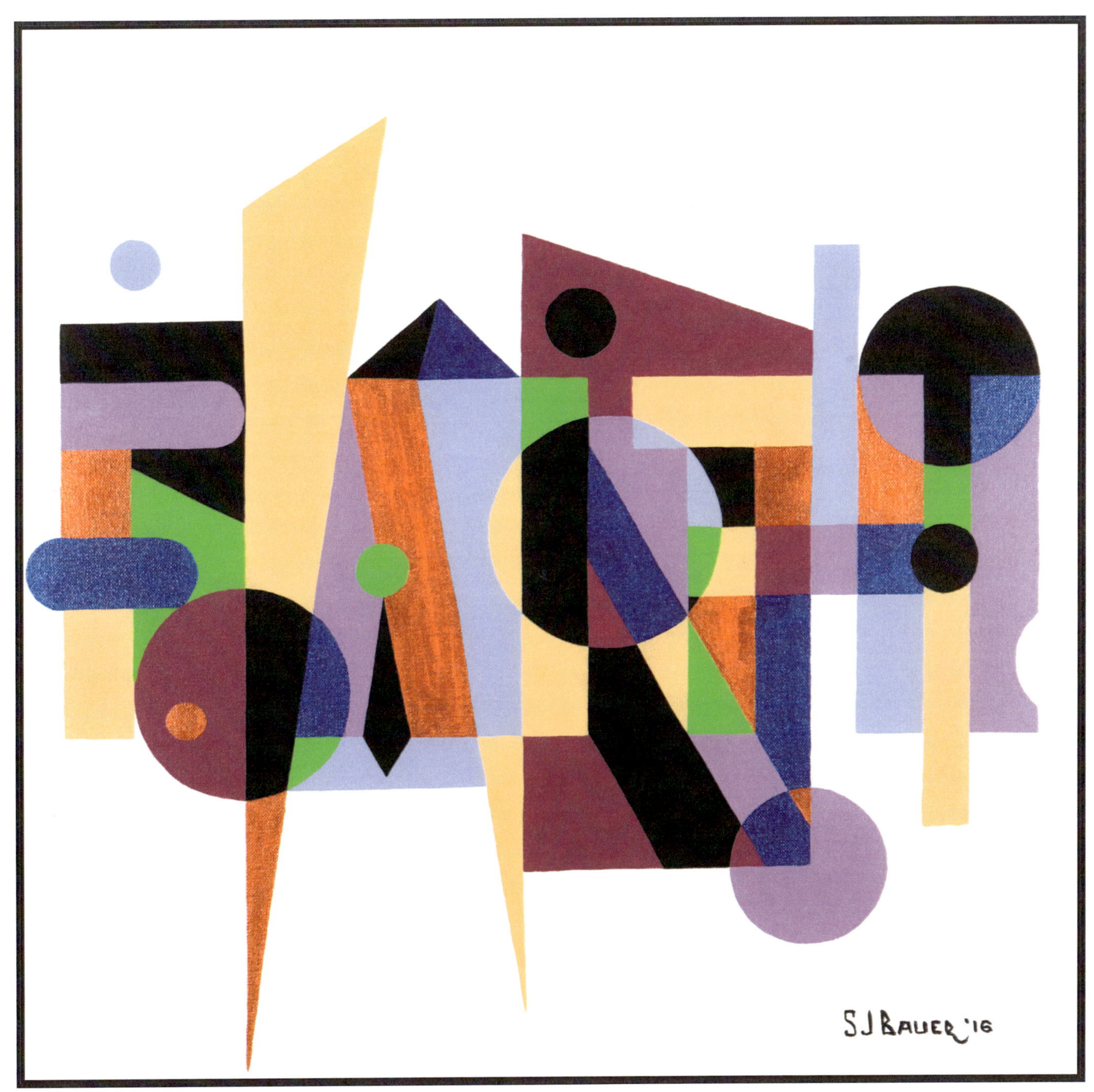

SJ BAUER '16

Someday.....

30" x 48" Acrylic on canvas

"Somebody should tell us, right at the start of our lives, that we are dying. Then we might live life to the limit, every minute of every day. Do it! I say. Whatever you want to do, do it now! There are only so many tomorrows."
Pope Paul VI

"Procrastination gives you time to consider divergent ideas, to think in nonlinear ways, to make unexpected leaps."
Adam Grant

"When you find yourself on the Internet when you're supposed to be writing, you've already lost. It's even beyond procrastination when you end up on the Internet."
Noah Baumbach

"A good procrastination should feel like you're inserting lots and lots of commas into the sentence of your life."
Ze Frank

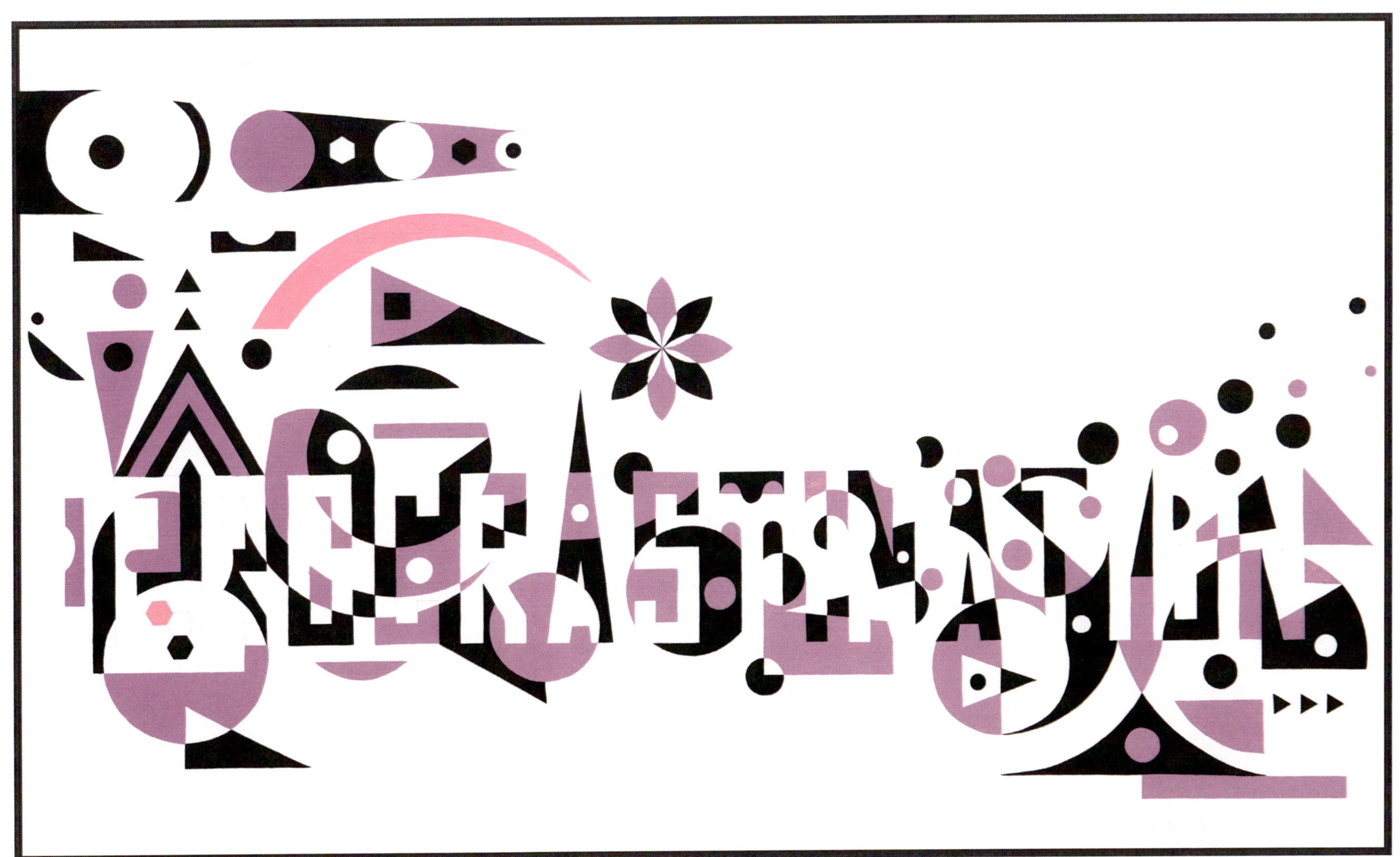
PROCRASTINATION

Don't Rush It

36" x 36" Acrylic on canvas

"Patience is not simply the ability to wait - it's how we behave while we're waiting."
Joyce Meyer

"The trees that are slow to grow bear the best fruit."
Moliere

"Patience and perseverance have a magical effect before which difficulties disappear and obstacles vanish."
John Quincy Adams

"Patience, n. A minor form of dispair, disguised as a virtue."
Ambrose Bierce

"Patience is a virtue, and I'm learning patience. It's a tough lesson."
Elon Musk

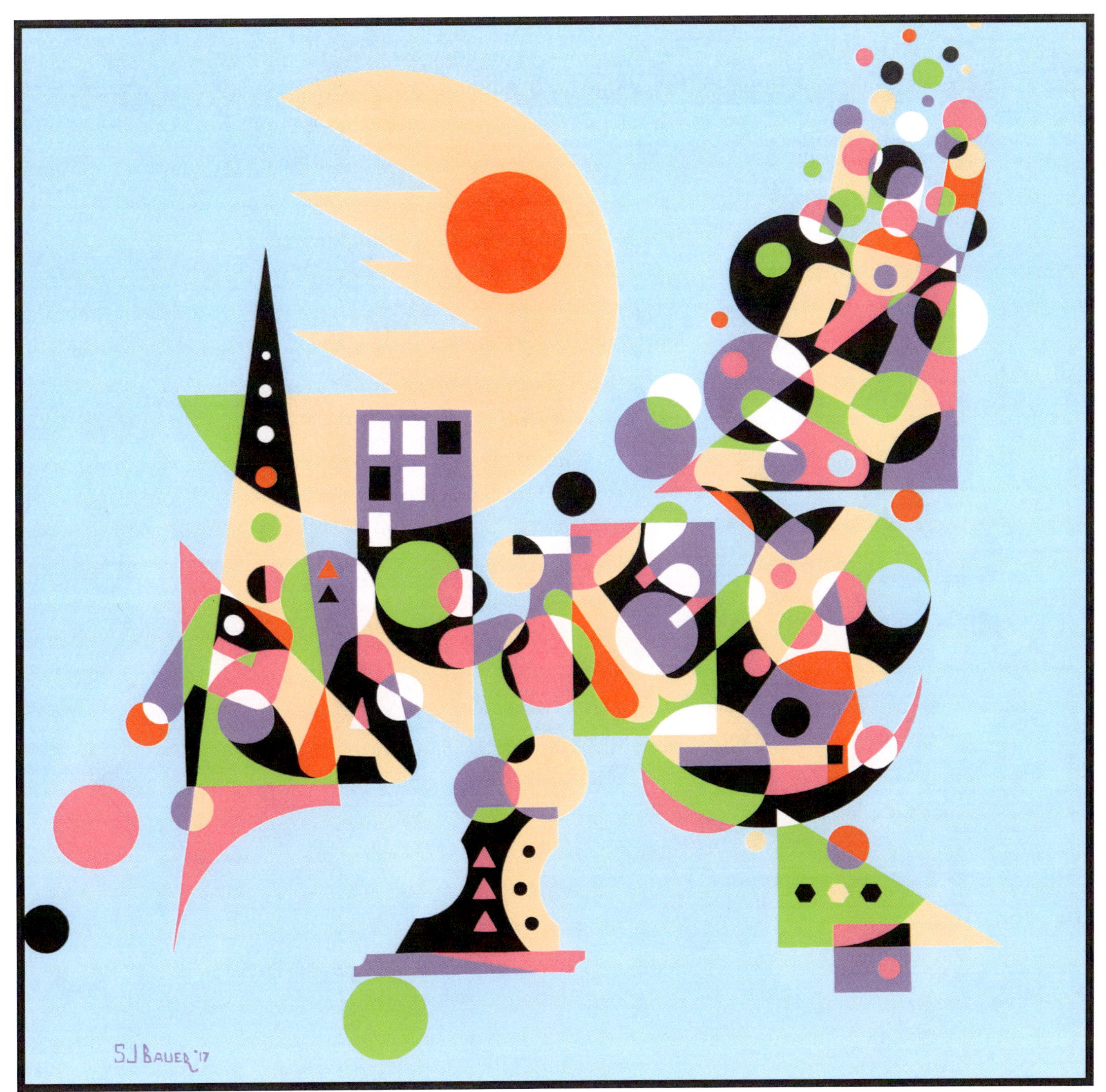

SJ BAUER '17

I Know What You Are Going Through

36" x 36" Acrylic on canvas

"Learning to stand in somebody else's shoes, to see through their eyes, that's how peace begins. And it's up to you to make that happen. Empathy is a quality of character that can change the world."
Barack Obama

"I do not ask the wounded person how he feels, I myself become the wounded person."
Walt Whitman

"When you show deep empathy toward others, their defensive energy goes down, and positive energy replaces it. That's when you can get more creative in solving problems."
Stephen Covey

"Empathy is really the opposite of spiritual meanness. It's the capacity to understand that every war is both won and lost. And that someone else's pain is as meaningful as your own."
Barbara Kingsolver

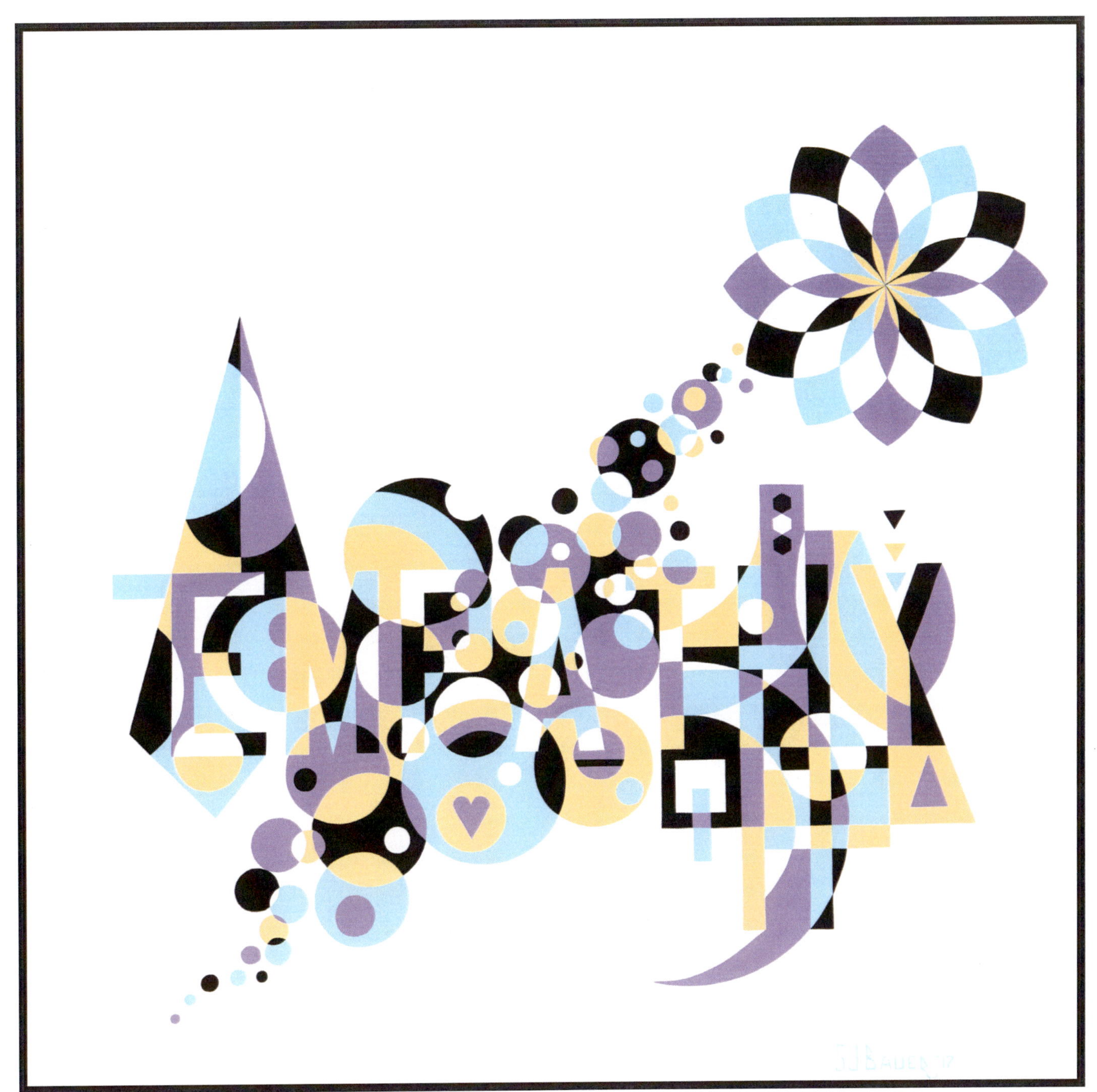

Howdy!

24" x 30" Mixed media on canvas

"In the Bible, shalom means universal flourishing, wholeness, and delight--a rich state of affairs in which natural needs are satisfied and natural gifts fruitfully employed, a state of affairs that inspires joyful wonder as its Creator and Savior opens doors and welcomes the creatures in whom he delights. Shalom, in other words, is the way things ought to be."
Cornelius Plantinga

"Koran says whoever believes in God in the last day shall be saved. It is a religion whose very name, Islam, comes from the word Shalom, which means peace. It's about establishing peace. We greet each other with peace be upon you, which the Jews do in greeting each other."
Feisal Abdul Rauf

"A society concerned with shalom will care for the most marginalized among them. God has a special concern for the poor and needy, because how we treat them reveals our hearts, regardless of the rhetoric we employ to make ourselves sound just."
Randy S. Woodley

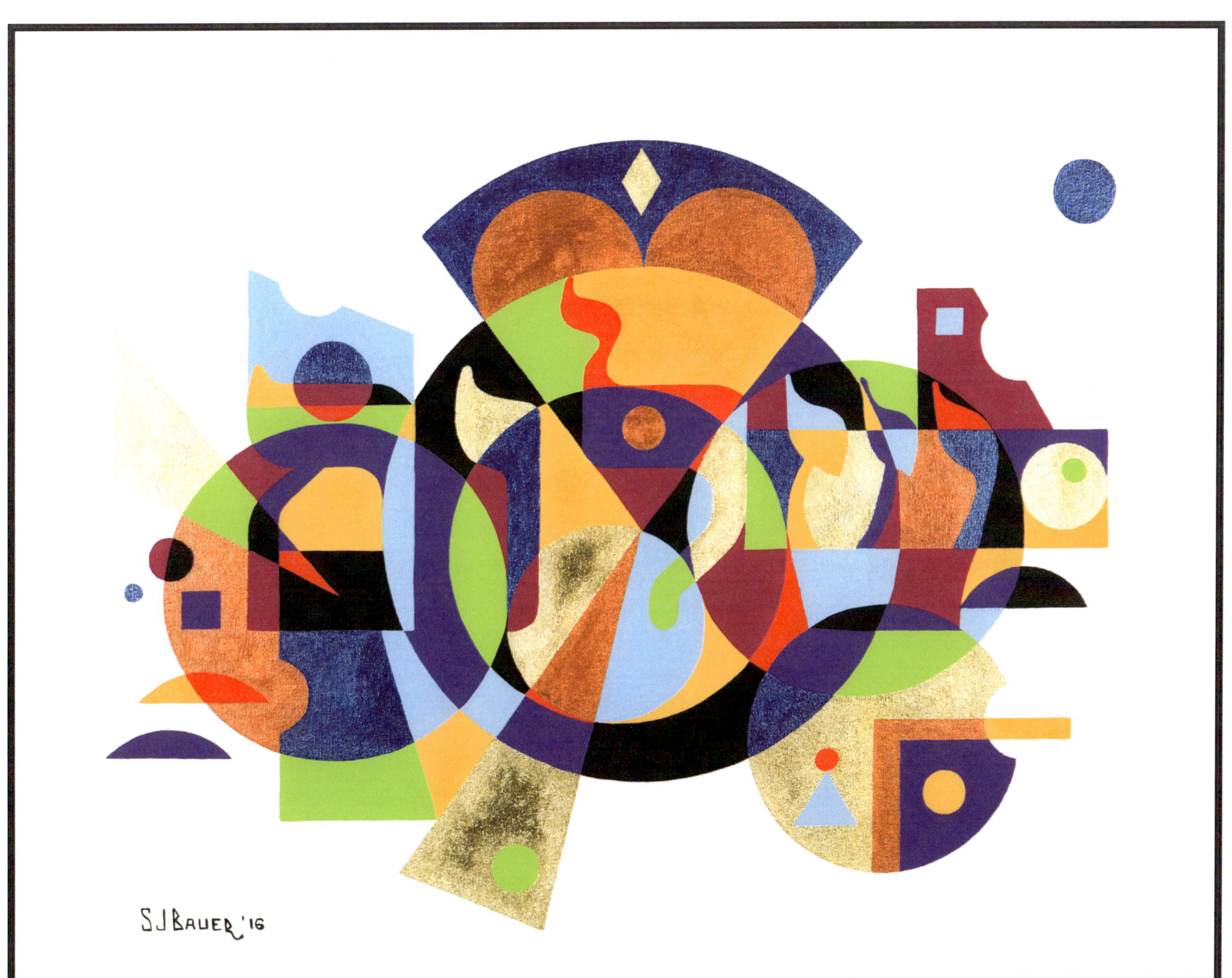

SJBauer '16

We're on the Same Page

24" x 30" Acrylic on canvas

"Friendship is one mind in two bodies."
Mencius

"Christ wasn't a Christian and Buddha wasn't a Buddhist and Muhammad wasn't Muslim. These people were having the experience of unity consciousnesses and universal consciousness and they spoke of it in words."
Deepak Chopra

"A cell in our body may recognize that it is part of a greater whole, but it may never be able to define all that is beyond it simply because of its limited perceptive capacity. Likewise, all that makes up the universal consciousness will always lie just outside of our capacity to define it."
Rajeev Kurapati

"The operative idea here is that there is a right and wrong theology
a right God and a wrong God. But this is an invalid premise.
All versions of God are the same thing: a human intertpretation of the universal consciousness"
Carlton D. Pearson

If You Build It

36" x 48" Acrylic on canvas

"The creative adult is the child who has survived."
Ursula K. Le Guin

"Imagination is the beginning of creation. You imagine what you desire, you will what you imagine and at last you create what you will."
George Bernard Shaw

"The delicate balance of mentoring someone is not creating them in your own image, but giving them the opportunity to create themselves."
Steven Spielberg

"By believing passionately in something that still does not exist, we create it. The nonexistent is whatever we have not sufficiently desired."
Franz Kafka

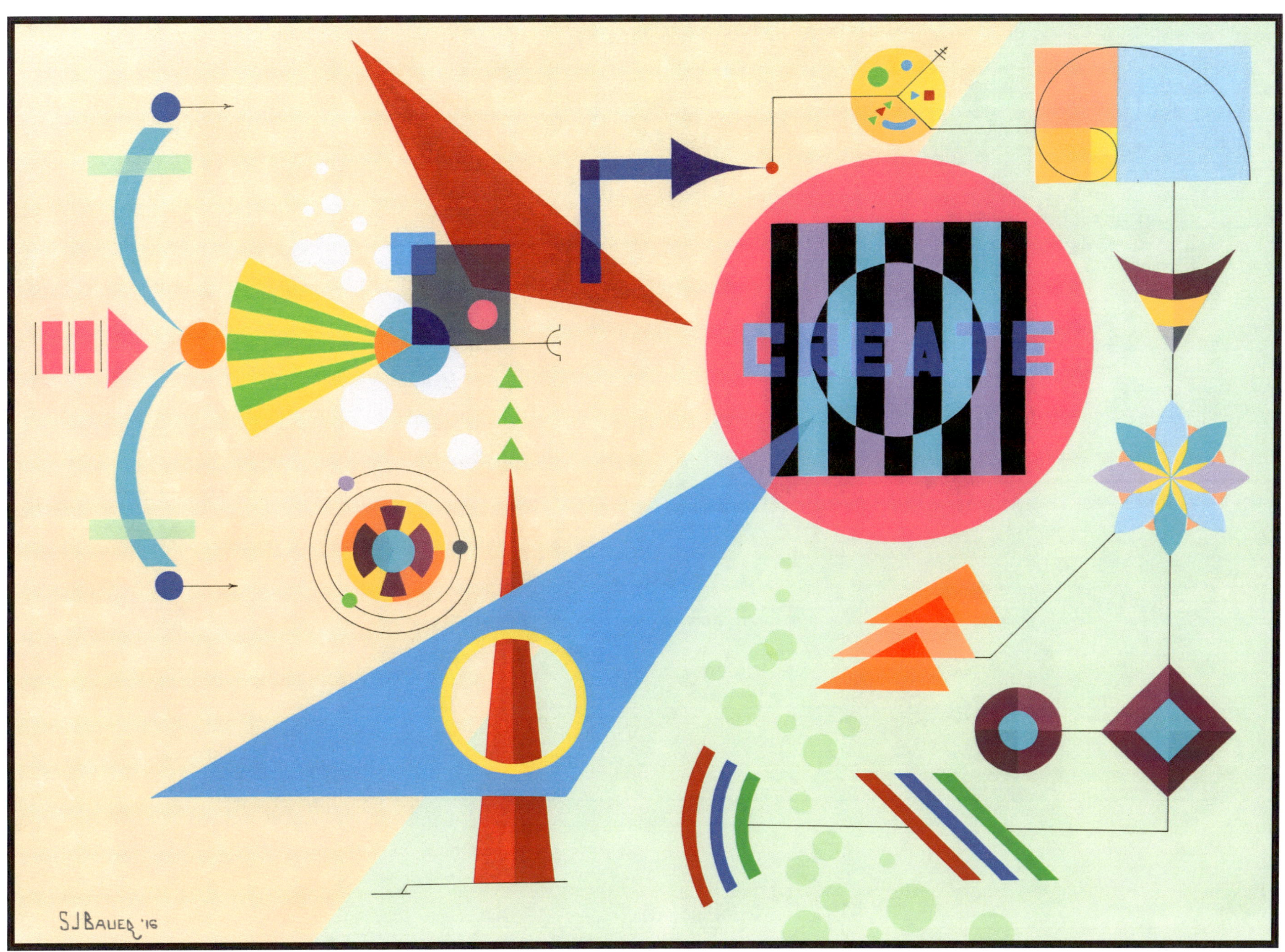

CREATE
SJ BAUER '16

I Would Not Lie

24" x 36" Acrylic on canvas

"Truth allows you to live with integrity. Everything you do and say shows the world who you really are. Let it be the Truth."
Oprah Winfrey

"Never be afraid to raise your voice for honesty and truth and compassion against injustice and lying and greed. If people all over the world...would do this, it would change the earth."
William Faulkner

"We are all travelers in the wilderness of this world, and the best we can find in our travels is an honest friend."
Robert Louis Stevenson

"The trite saying that honesty is the best policy has met with the just criticism that honesty is not policy. The real honest man is honest from conviction of what is right, not from policy."
Robert E. Lee

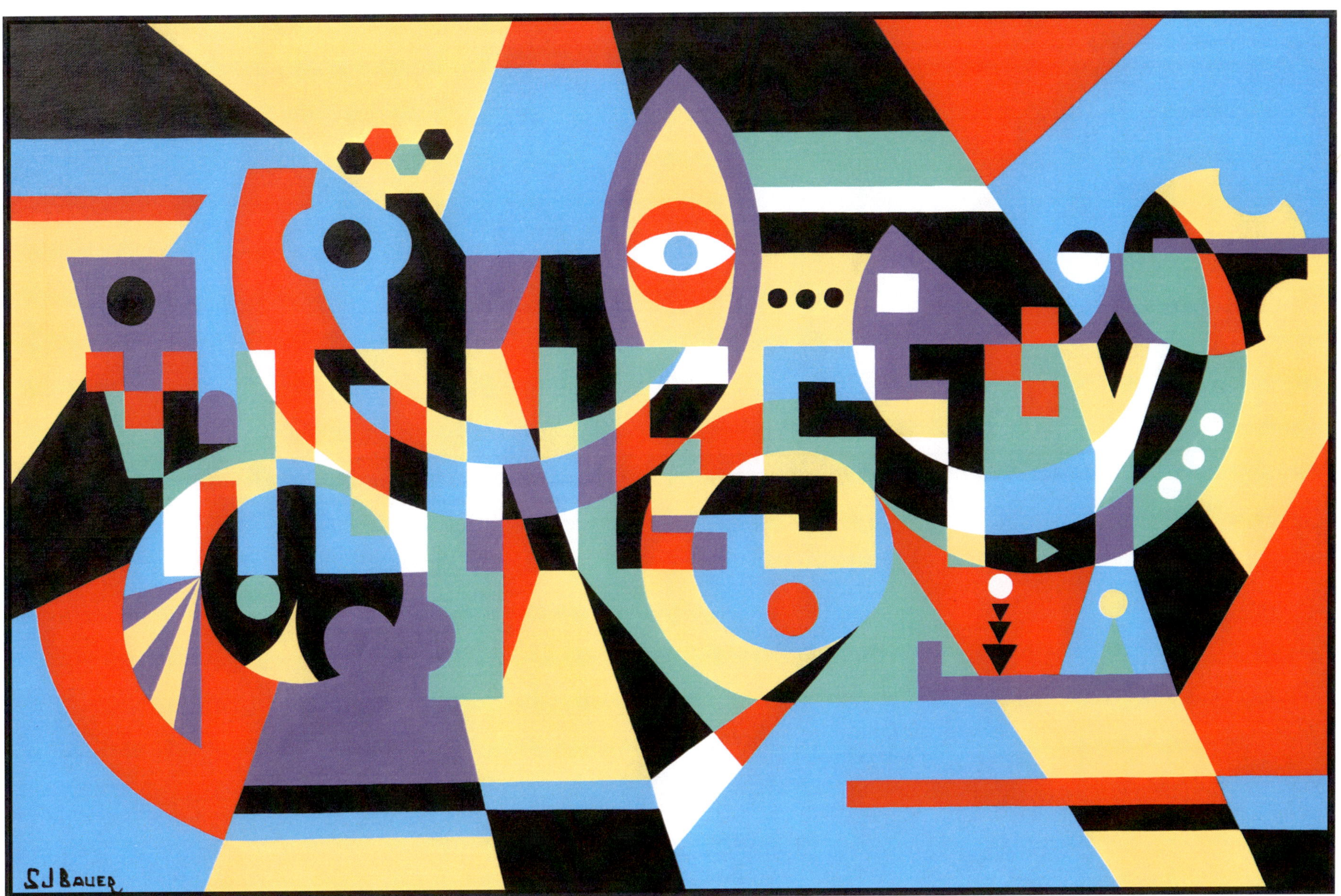

HONESTY
SJ BAUER

I Will Follow You Anywhere

30" x 40" Acrylic on canvas

"Trust is earned, respect is given, and loyalty is demonstrated. Betrayal of any one of those is to lose all three."
Ziad K. Abdelnour

"Animals are reliable, many full of love, true in their affections, predictable in their actions, grateful and loyal. Difficult standards for people to live up to."
Alfred Armand Montapert

"You cannot buy loyalty; you cannot buy the devotion of hearts, minds, and souls. You have to earn these things."
Clarence Francis

"I have a loyalty that runs in my bloodstream, when I lock into someone or something, you can't get me away from it because I commit that thoroughly. That's in friendship, that's a deal, that's a commitment. Don't give me paper - I can get the same lawyer who drew it up to break it. But if you shake my hand, that's for life."
Jerry Lewis

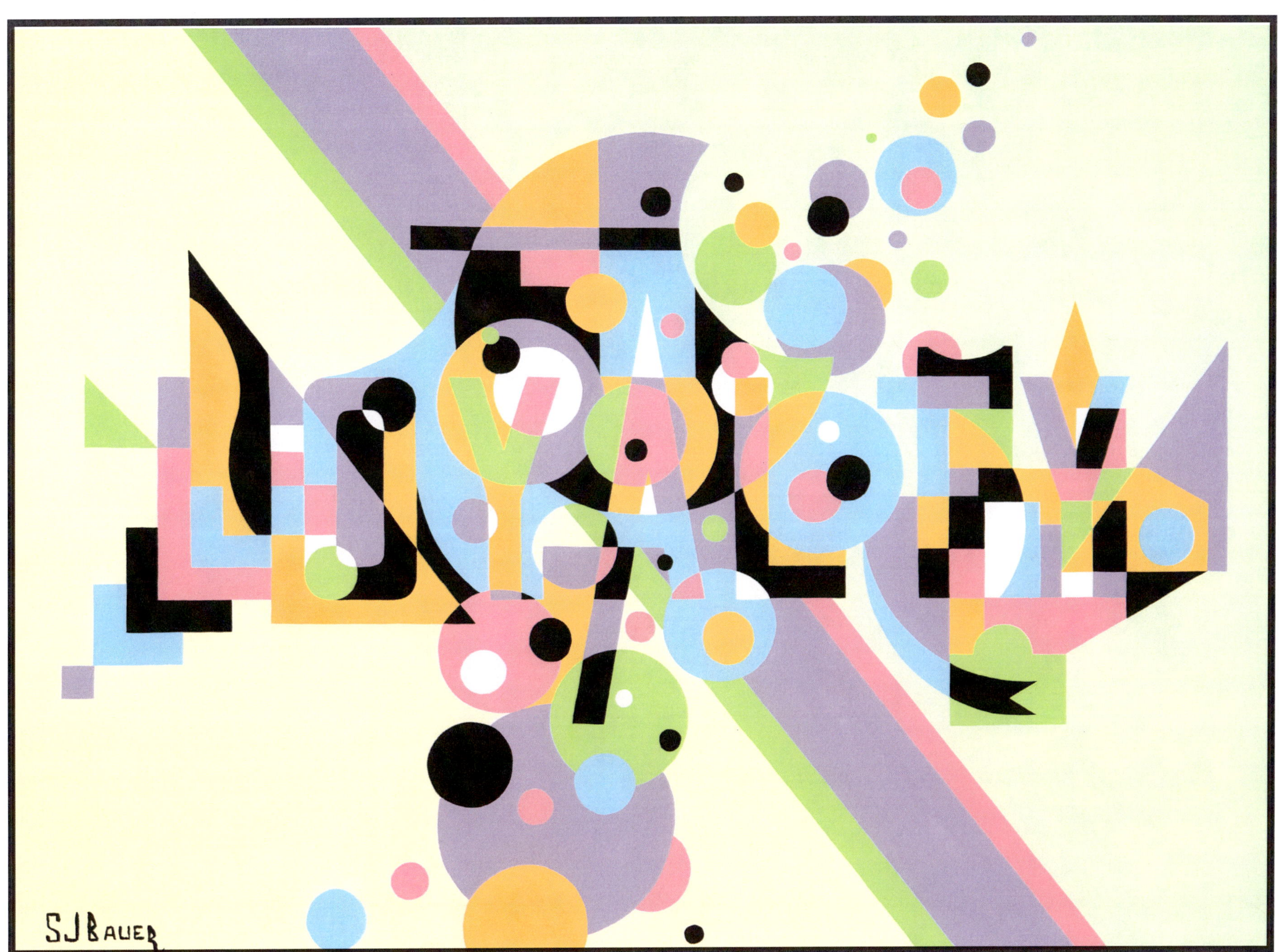
LOYALTY
SJ BAUER

Make Yourself At Home

48" x 60" Acrylic on canvas

"Hospitality means we take people into the space that is our lives and our minds and our hearts and our work and our efforts. Hospitality is the way we come out of ourselves. It is the first step towards dismantling the barriers of the world. Hospitality is the way we turn a prejudiced world around, one heart at a time."
Joan D. Chittister

"True Hospitality is welcoming the stranger on her own terms. This kind of hospitality can only be offered by those who've found the center of their lives in their own hearts."
Henri Nouwen

"Certainly I have found, as many travellers before me, that people in the poorest places are often the readiest to shower me, from an affluent country, with hospitality and kindness."
Pico Iyer

"In the cherry blossom's shade there's no such thing as a stranger."
Kobayashi Issa

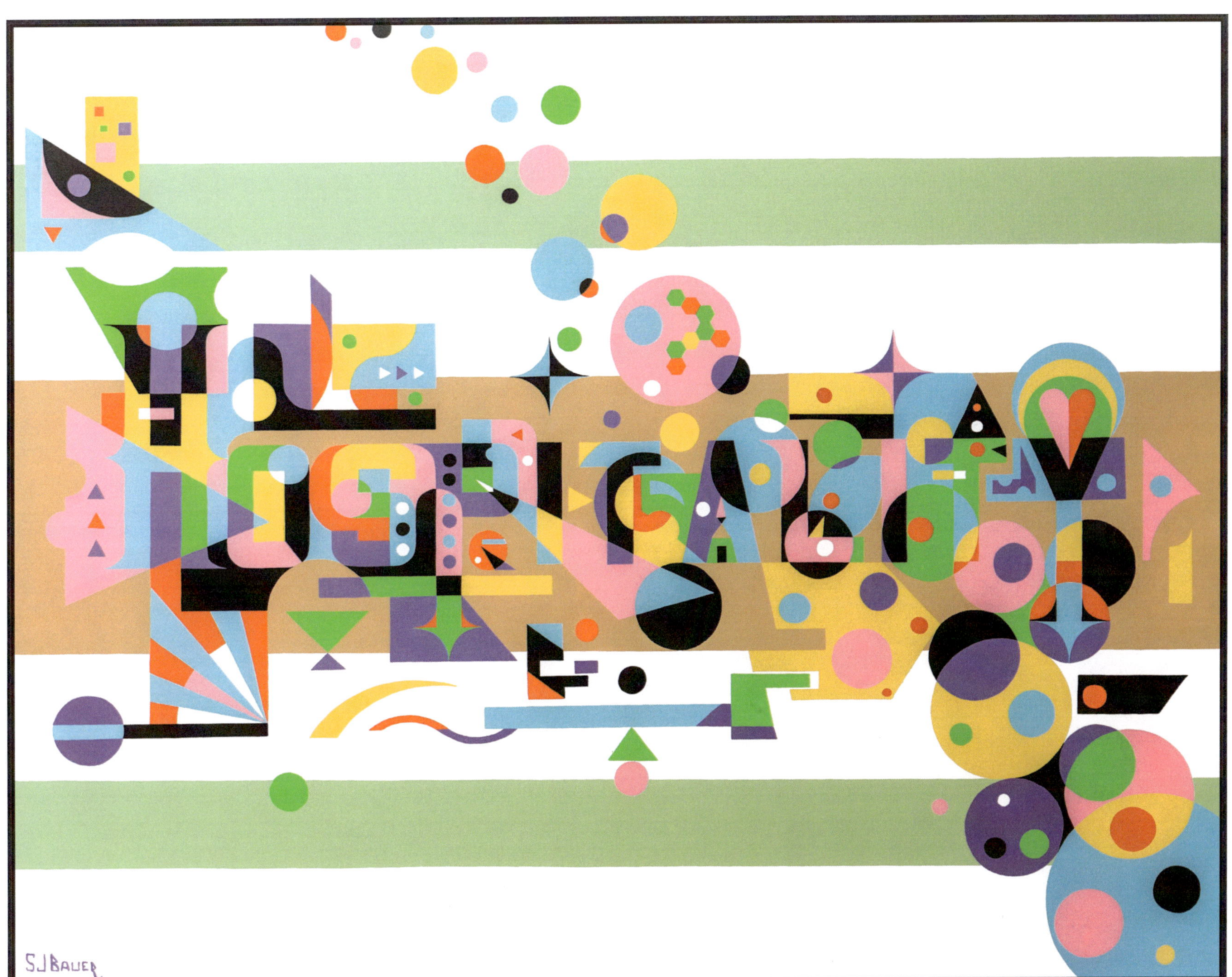

SJ BAUER

Take it Easy

24" x 30" Acrylic on canvas

"Your mind will answer most questions if you learn to relax and wait for the answer."
William S. Burroughs

"The time to relax is when you don't have time for it."
Sydney J. Harris

"Whenever in doubt, turn off your mind, relax, and float downstream."
John Lennon

"Golf's ultimate moral instruction directs us to find within ourselves a pivotal center of enjoyment: relax into a rhythm that fits the hills and swales, and play the shot at hand - not the last one, or the next one, but the one at your feet, in the poison ivy, where you put it."
John Updike

"Tension is who you think you should be. Relaxation is who you are."
Chinese Proverb

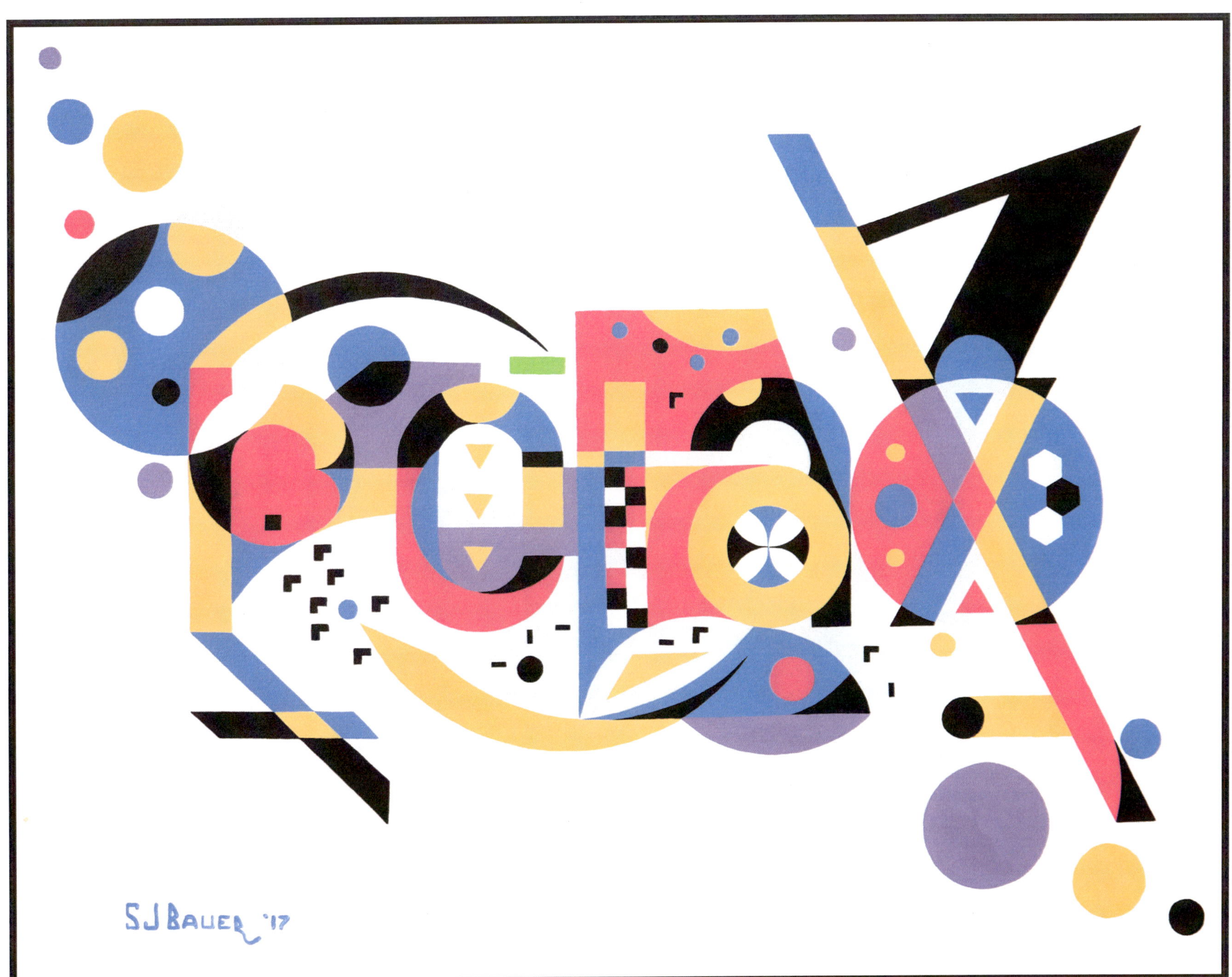

Fresh Air

24" x 30" Acrylic on canvas

"When you arise in the morning, think of what a precious privilege it is to be alive - to breathe, to think, to enjoy, to love."
Marcus Aurelius

"Breathe. Let go. And remind yourself that this very moment is the only one you know you have for sure."
Oprah Winfrey

"You cannot breathe deeply and worry at the same time. Breathe. Let the worry go. Breathe. Allow the love and intuition in."
Sonia Choquette

"For in the final analysis, our most basic common link is that we all inhabit this small planet. We all breathe the same air. We all cherish our children's futures. And we are all mortal."
John F. Kennedy

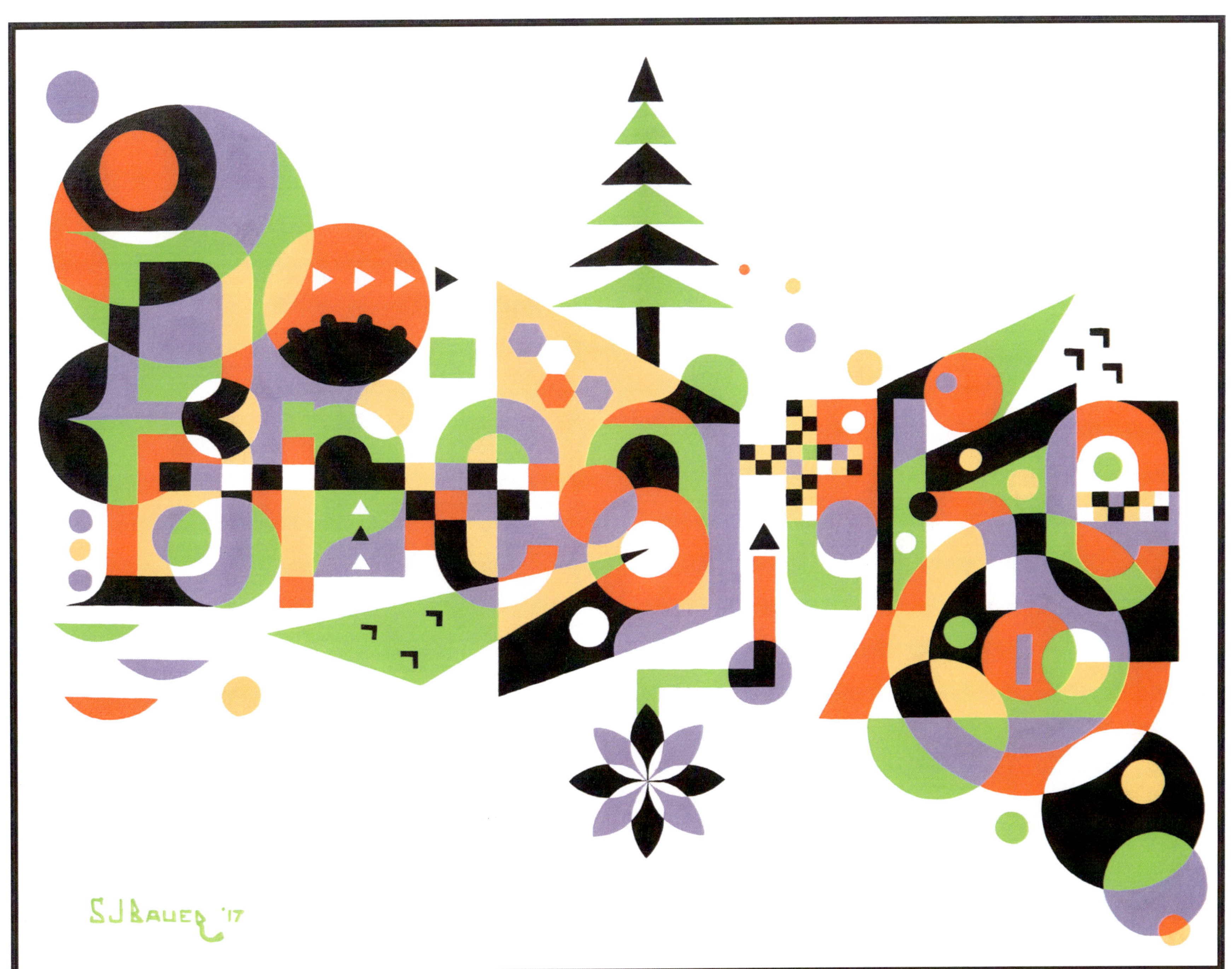

SJ Bauer '17

Index of Paintings

Page Number	**Painting Title**	**Word**
56	I Feel Ya	Compassion
58	Live And Let Live	Manifest Tolerance
60	I Really Mean It	Sincerity
62	Springs Eternal	Hope
64	We Are All The Same	Equality
66	Key To The Universe	Believe
68	You Are Better Than This	Rise Above
70	What Goes Around	Kindness
72	Give Til It Hurts	Generosity
74	It's All You Need	Love
76	Sock It To Me	Respect
78	We're Stronger Together	United We Stand
80	Lead by Example	Inspire
82	I Don't Need Proof	Faith
84	Some Day…..	Procrastination
86	Don't Rush It	Patience
88	I Know What You Are Going Through	Empathy
90	Howdy!	Shalom (in Hebrew)
92	We Are On The Same Page	One Mind
94	If You Build It	Create
96	I Would Not Lie	Honesty
98	I Will Follow You Anywhere	Loyalty
100	Make Yourself At Home	Hospitality
102	Take It Easy	Relax
104	Fresh Air	Breathe

The Safe Nest Mural Project

As an extension of the Art of Inspiration Project, I wanted to do a wall mural, out of my pocket, for charity. I chose Safe Nest shelter for abused women and children, a cause I feel strongly about. A dear friend of mine, Patrick Duffy, CEO of the Nevada School of the Arts, introduced me to his friend Liz Wheeler, CEO of Safe Nest, and went to the first meeting with me to help pitch the project. I decided that I wanted to do the word "Hope" as I thought it was the one thing that everyone who went through those doors had in common. Liz was very positive about the idea and was elated that I had chosen the word "Hope." Unbeknownst to me, hope is a very important word at the shelter. Liz told me that the shelter uses a hope scale developed at the University of Oklahoma to gauge a client's chance of success in being able to break the chain of abuse and make their life better. She gave us a tour of one of their facilities and we chose a wall in the dining hall for the location of the mural. The wall in the dining hall was painted a dark purple color which gave the room a dark and somewhat dreary feel. I knew I could surely change that.

Work began a couple weeks later. I had to dig into some of my old skills to skim coat and sand the wall using drywall mud to remove the texture and give a suitable surface to paint on. I had forgotten how physically arduous that kind of work was. Easy at twenty five, much more painful at sixty five. Two days of troweling mud and sanding had the wall

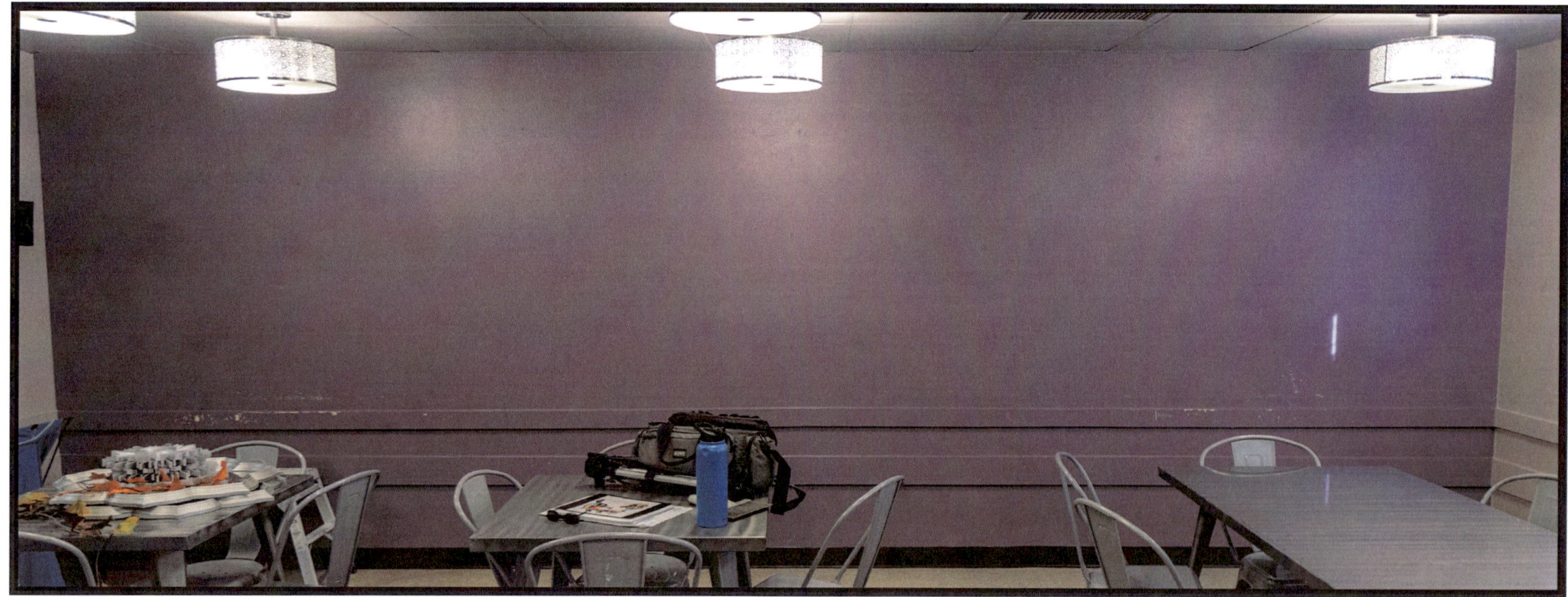

ready for primer and a coat of white paint. That change alone made a world of difference in the character of the room. I decided to create a three piece mural. The center part would be the word "Hope". On each side of that I would make an interactive panel where residents could express their thoughts and be engaged directly in the mural project. I wanted this mural to be theirs, a part of who they are, and provide a platform to express their thoughts on Hope and their experience at the shelter. The panel on the left was labeled "What Hope Means to Me" and the panel on the right was labeled "Messages of Hope to Future Residents."

I wanted the mural to be bright, colorful, and uplifting. I also wanted it to be tangibly functional in allowing residents to express their feelings to others in similar situations. Two days of layout and drawing and I was finally able to begin the fun part of painting the mural. Reaction from the residents was immediate and positive. They loved the bright cheerful colors and were impressed by how much the character of the room changed, even as the painting was in progress.

Actual painting of the mural took about a week. During this time I had the opportunity to get to know some of the residents and hear a bit about their personal

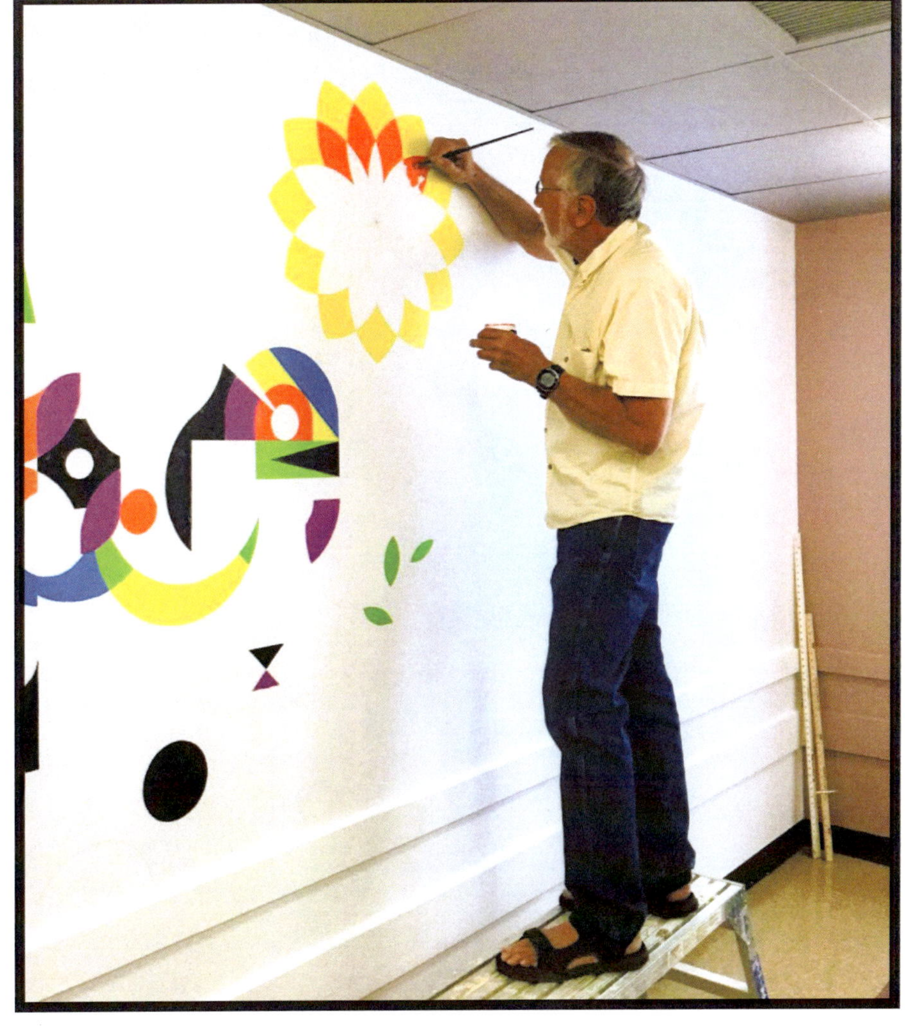

stories. I have to say that getting to know these people was one of the most uplifting experiences of my life. The bravery to do what they had done, uprooting their life, gathering up their children, leaving what little support structure they had behind, and to carry on in the hope that they were doing the right thing and that everything would work out for the better, was truly inspirational. These women stepped off a cliff with little more than hope and faith that Safe Nest would be able to guide them to a better existence free of abuse and fear. I'm not sure I would have the strength to do that if I were in their place.

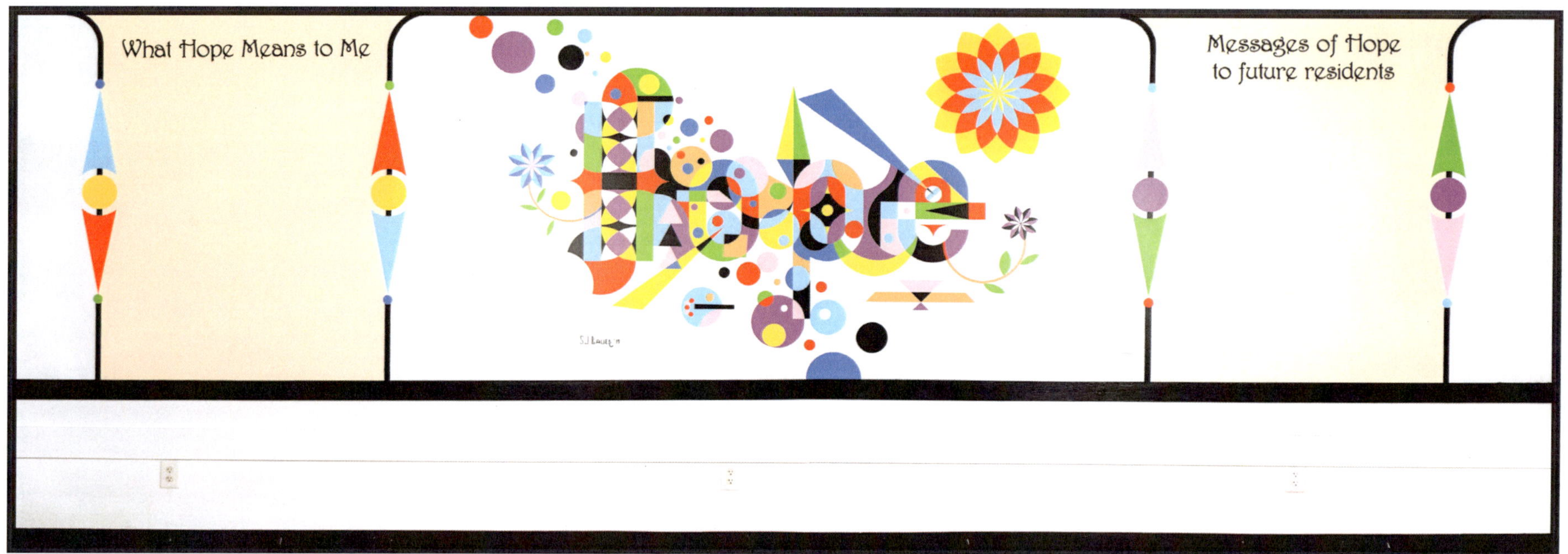

In a little under two weeks total time, the project was finished. The transformation of energy in the room was remarkable. Everyone involved was thrilled, including myself. My work is a constant source of amazement for me. I always wonder where the inspiration and designs for my paintings come from. I stand in front of a blank canvas, or wall in this case, and it just flows out of me. The source is a mystery. Sometimes I feel I am channelling the art from somewhere outside myself. In this case, however, I believe it came from the heart. The people I interacted with boosted me to greater heights, and I think this is one of my best works.

I finished the project by placing a "message from the artist" sign on the adjacent wall which explained my motives for making the mural and my desire that residents use it as a platform to express their feelings to others around them. The sign read as follows:

Message From the Artist

When I decided to donate a wall mural to charity, I wanted to do a word painting as an extension of my "Art of Inspiration" project. I selected Safe Nest because it is a cause I truly believe in. No one should be forced to live a life of abuse, fear, and pain. I selected the word "Hope" because I thought it was the one thing that everyone who walked through these doors had in common.

This mural is a gift from me to you, the residents of Safe Nest, and I want you all to be a part of it. Everyone here has a story to tell. I added a panel at each end of the mural where residents can pen their thoughts about hope. The left panel is titled "What Hope means to me." This is the space where you can let others know how hope affects you, how you define it, or what you hope to achieve here. The right side panel is titled "Messages of Hope to future residents". This is where you can help someone else who is just coming into this system through your experience. Remember when you showed up on this doorstep alone, afraid, and full of doubt? What would you tell yourself looking back?

I hope that these spaces will be used in a positive manner with love and compassion for others in your situation. This is your opportunity to pay it forward. Think carefully about what you would like to write and how you will word it as your thoughts or advice will be permanent for all to see for as long as this mural is here. Try to keep comments brief to allow space for others who will write things later. Sign your work.

I feel blessed to have had the opportunity to meet some of you in my short time at the shelter. I love you all and pray that all of you find whatever it is you are hoping for.

As a last gesture, I penned my own thoughts on the interactive panels. In the What Hope Means to Me panel I wrote:

"When surrounded by darkness, hope provides the strength and determination to find our way back into the light".

In the Messages of Hope To Future Residents panel I wrote:

"Hope has brought you to this doorstep. Don't look back. For behind you lie only broken dreams. Ahead of you is where new dreams become real".

Leaving the shelter for the last time was bittersweet. I will miss the people I met there and the opportunity to personally interact with them. I'll miss my creation as I know I must leave it behind in this secure location. On the bright side, I left the residents here a piece of myself, a bit of my soul that I hope will inspire and help them, and future residents for years to come, to pursue the life they deserve, free from fear, pain, and abuse.

Hope

Wall Mural, 6' x 21', Interior eggshell latex wall paint

"God is the light. Faith is the path. Hope is the backpack we take on our journey."
SafeNest resident

"Hope gives me the strength to push through anything thrown my way. The strength to wake up every morning! YOU GOT THIS, KEEP YOUR HEAD HELD HIGH QUEEN!"
SafeNest Resident

"Hope is a pinnacle of resilience; it is the fuel to move us forward, providing a glimmer of optimism in times of trouble. With hope, we know tomorrow will be brighter than today."
Genese Jones-Torrence SafeNest VP

"Hope means to stay stronger than any negative. To be a fighter. To be a warrior!"
SafeNest Resident

"Today we close the door to the past and open the door to the future; take a deep breath, step on through and start a new chapter in your life."
SafeNest Resident

"Hope means having the strength, courage, and the will power to get out of a toxic environment so that you can the best person you can be for YOURSELF."
SafeNest Resident

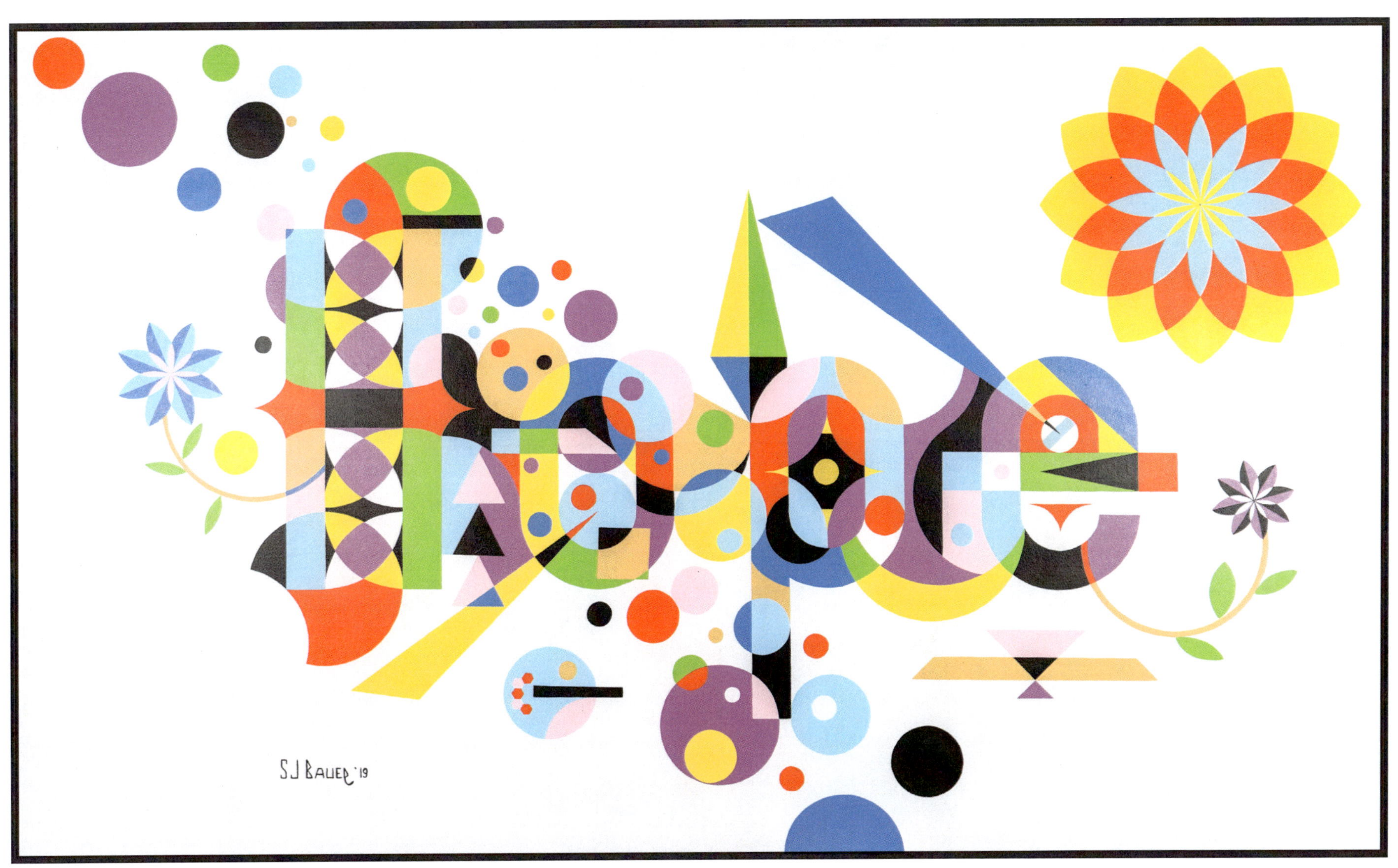

Hope
SJ Bauer '19

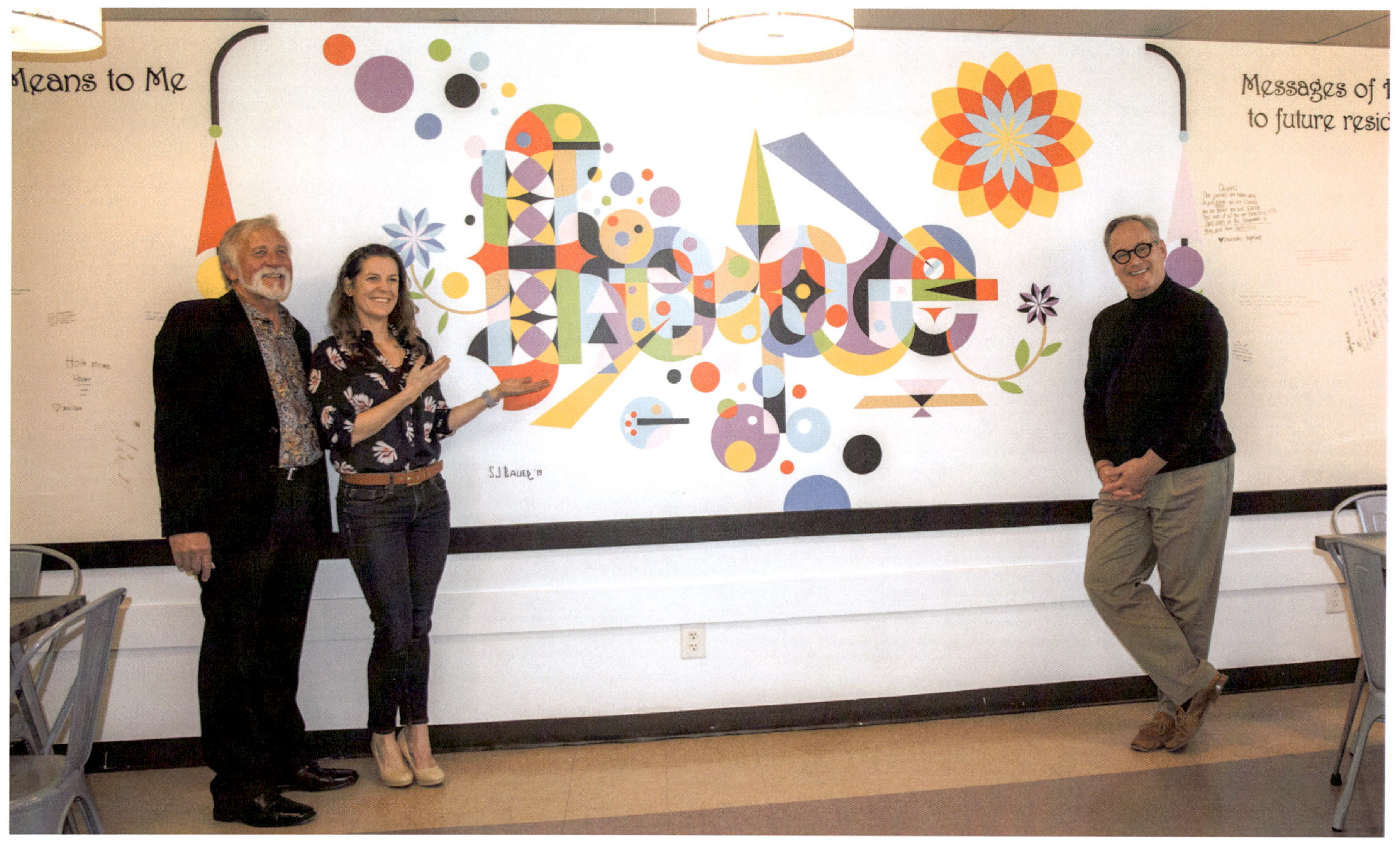

SafeNest Hope mural with (from left to right) Scott Bauer, artist; Liz Wheeler, CEO of Safenest; and Patrick Duffy, CEO Nevada School of the Arts.

Special thanks to Liz Wheeler and Patrick Duffy for their enthusiasm and support in making this project happen.